# Virginia's COUNTRY STORES
## a quiet passing

# Virginia's COUNTRY STORES

## a quiet passing

### AN ILLUSTRATED REMINISCENCE
### by Joseph E. Morse

## ACKNOWLEDGEMENTS

I am deeply indebted to my wife, who has traveled with me over countless miles of Virginia highways and byways in the seemingly endless search for country stores. She is also my sounding board as well as my typist. I am also delighted to give credit to my son, Adam, for setting this book in type. At the beginning of my quest, both Angus Green and Duff Green were extremely supportive of my efforts. My hat is off to the U.S. Postal Service personnel, who helped guide me to many fine old stores, and to Kevin Spain, who led me to stores I would never have found on my own. The greatest feeling of indebtedness I have is to the merchants who shared with me the memories of their stores during the "good ole days".

**Photographs and other Graphic materials unless otherwise credited are either by the author or from his collection.**

Copyright © 1996 by Joseph E. Morse
First Edition
All rights reserved. No part of this book may be reproduced or utilized in any form or by any means, electronic or mechanical, including photocopying, or by any information storage and retrieval system without permission in writing from the publisher.

ISBN: 1-880664-19-4
Library of Congress Catalog Card Number: 96-47597

E.M. Press, Inc.
P.O. Box 4057
Manassas, VA 20108

 _Cover_, A Country Store in Greene County as it appeared in the 1970s, _Frontispiece_, store of Boonesville, Albemarle County, _Foreword page_, store front in the town of Luray, _Contents page_, interior view of the General Store in Buena Vista.

# FOREWORD

As I explored the subject of Virginia country stores historically, I came to a disappointing conclusion. Since every city, town, village or crossroads supported at least one store, people behind the camera evidently felt no obligation or inclination to record them for posterity. They were too commonplace.

I have searched many printed Virginia town histories, photo collections, museums, antique shops, and newspapers and have uncovered very few store photographs. When a picture was located, it usually contained figures that managed to obliterate the store behind them, or was of such poor quality that it was not worth reproducing.

Of course, I uncovered conflagration shots that made front page news, but were of little use. That left me the option I chose for this publication. Record what is out there, what remains.

I began this quest almost 30 years ago. Over that period of time, I've watched stores close down and buildings disappear. Recently, traveling to both familiar and unexplored areas around the state, I found a surprising number of those quiet country roads are becoming four-lane highways, with new homes on either side. Once derelict store buildings have blossomed under shiny new siding in decorator colors, with large canopied gas pumps out front and a "general line" of merchandise inside. Yes, the "general store" has made a comeback in a limited fashion. But the true country stores, as well as the merchants who ran them, are history.

# INTRODUCTION

My first contact with a country store came when I was eight years old. My dad purchased a lot in a small resort on the Chesapeake Bay which had been a tobacco plantation until the late 1800s. What remained was the manor house, acres of exhausted soil, a lovely stretch of white sandy beach, and a long wooden pier that at one time held iron tracks which carried tobacco hogsheads out to deep water for sailing ships.

Near the beach, adjacent to the pier, was a very old, weathered building open only during the summer as a country store. Stock was limited to bare necessities for the small resort community springing up nearby.

The floorboards in the store had warped, leaving spaces between large enough for sand and soil to be seen underneath. A dropped coin was lost forever. The shelves sagged so badly that items placed along them usually slipped to the center of the sag.

Each day required at least two trips to the store to buy a penny's worth of candy and watch the occasional customer come and go. A vivid picture of the old store has remained with me.

My great affection for the country store developed in the middle 1960s. My wife and I decided to move our young but growing family from the ever-expanding suburbs to the wide open spaces of rural Virginia, to surroundings similar to those in which we had been raised. We found a comfortable older home with a few acres in a small village, and as fate would have it, only a stone's throw from an old country store.

This was a true general store. It had gas pumps out front, a complete line of groceries at not quite supermarket prices, local produce in season, and on occasion, fresh, home-grown beef and pork.

The paints and hardware were brand-name products, and the clothing for men, women and children was astonishingly good. At Christmas time, a whole section of the store was filled with Christmas toys and other presents. After the city, it was hard to believe, all your Christmas shopping was at one location!

It wasn't long before my interest in country stores began to lead me along the roads of our neighboring countryside. I then decided it might be wise to keep a record of stores visited and photograph them if possible. For approximately 30 years, I have logged countless miles, on a variety of vehicles, exploring the highways and rural byways of Virginia and discovering country stores. Many I photographed, but I found a number of structures that were not as pictorially interesting or were too similar and passed by. On other occasions, I didn't have a camera with me and missed recording a few good buildings.

Many general stores I found were closed. Others opened part-time and were fill-in stores selling soft drinks, cigarettes and such. Only 10 or 12 were true country general stores. Of the stores that remained open, I accidentally discovered that four within a 50-mile radius were operated by octogenarians. To find an old store still open was to find a little segment of history remaining intact. I could walk in and immediately be transported back in time. The look, the smells, little had been changed by the intervening years - not two World Wars, not the Depression. Proof was often right there in front of me.

Having spent my adult life shopping up-to-the-minute city and suburban businesses, finding an old store with merchandise that had been on the shelf since the time of Teddy Roosevelt or Woodrow Wilson staggered my imagination and kept me searching.

When the merchants realized I was not a dealer seeking items for resale, but was genuinely interested in the store's history, they were most cooperative. Much of the lore of storekeeping and the anecdotes told to me I've included in this text, all with the sole purpose of helping to chronicle Virginia's almost gone, but lovingly remembered country stores.

# TABLE OF CONTENTS

*chapter* **1** ORIGIN OF COUNTRY STORES, THEIR RISE & DECLINE . . . . . . . . . . . . pg. 5

*chapter* **2** THE BUSINESS OF TENDING A GENERAL STORE . . . . . . . . . . . . . . . pg. 13

*chapter* **3** THE LIGHTER SIDE OF STOREKEEPING . . . . . . . . . . . . . . . . . pg. 27

**OLD STORES: A Picture Album** . . . . . . . . . . . pg. 33

*chapter* **4** RECREATING AN OLD COUNTRY STORE . . . . . . . . . . . . . . . . . pg. 101

**A COUNTRY STORE SCRAP BOOK** . . . . . . . pg. 106

INDEX TO STORE LOCATIONS . . . . . . . . . . . . pg. 128

*Colonial merchant-traders negotiating with Indians.*

# CHAPTER 1  ORIGIN OF COUNTRY STORES THEIR RISE AND DECLINE

The country general store is truly an American invention or innovation. On this, most historians are in agreement. But the where, why, and how are still disputed. One prominent theory contends that the Indians were responsible. It was their insistence that trading posts be furnished with all of their needs in one location, to make trading more convenient and efficient for them.

It logically began with planners of the early colonizing expeditions to the New World. They provided everything the colonists would need to survive for a given length of time aboard ship or ships. When they reached the New World, they constructed a building to hold the ships' "stores" and placed it at a central location for the convenience of all.

The *Virginia Historical Register* stated, in an article entitled "Virginia in 1616", details of the inner workings of the colony:

> "...the Councell and Company for Virginia have already sent a ship thither, furnished with all manner of clothing, household stuff and such necessaries to establish a magazin [store] there, which the people shall buy at easie rates for their commodities."
>
> "...the laborers are of two sorts. Some employed only in the generall works, who are fedd and clothed out of the store..." *

This concept was contrary to the merchandising customs of the Old World. A typical market in a small town or city held many merchants, each with his own special commodity. The general merchant was unknown.

The country general merchant was born of necessity. He played a much larger role in the formation of our free market economy than history has given him credit for. This New World was a vast, uncharted, undeveloped continent. There was no established order, political, social or economic. Everything had to be started from scratch: land cleared, crude living shelters erected, and

*The Virginia Historical Register, Volume 1, Number III, July 1848.

*An old-time French market for butter, eggs, and cheese.*

*Pack train crossing the mountains.*

some sources found for providing vital supplies or necessities settlers could not grow or make for themselves. The merchant-trader was born.

Collecting produce and/or items settlers grew or made that exceeded their own needs, the merchant-trader found markets for this excess with the Indians or other settlers.

In the early times, settlers, by necessity, traveled great distances for supplies. As more and more settlers arrived, communities emerged. A man with some "book learning", a little cash and an enterprising spirit, who perhaps had been a merchant-trader, might have become a general merchant. Using the five-mile radius rule-of-thumb for possible customers, he would have chosen a good location and built his country general store.

Another important consideration was how close the store site was to a supply route.

Virginia's rivers, and later canals, formed the most extensive and dependable network of transportation from early settlement well into the late 1800s. Cities and towns of today sit on the banks of streams that once were swift-flowing rivers carrying boats and barges filled with produce for markets throughout the state and beyond.

By the Civil War era, railroads began to rival water transport, and later in the century rendered it obsolete. This opened vast new areas for settlement and commerce. Even the mountainous regions were conquered by the rails. Many large country stores were located adjacent to railroad tracks, as were a number of 19th Century homes.

By 1900, railroads had become the most dependable source of transportation and supply, but it would be the 1920s, and the increasing ownership of automobiles, that would finally demand the construction of highways. Even the railroads campaigned on behalf of better roads to enable more farmers to get their products to railroad depots.

With modern highways came the beginning of the end for country general stores. At first, this helped the country merchant as roads brought customers and supplies more quickly and in greater variety. But the availability of better autos at affordable prices, and an ever-increasing network of highways, put more families on the road to bigger communities that offered specialty stores and cheaper prices.

At the end of World War II, maintaining a policy of credit to customers was the last hope of most country merchants. Those that remained open usually down-sized to a convenience store with an extremely limited selection. I found that a few even remain today.

One of my journeys was to an old store on a dusty, single lane road. After several attempts, I finally found it open. Finishing my chat with the aged proprietor, I decided to get a candy bar for the trip back home. On the road, I opened it. I shouldn't have. It was a true antique.

*In little more than 100 years, transportation in America progressed from the centuries-old method of pack animals (wood engraving opposite page) to the automobile, as illustrated by advertisements (right) from contemporary Virginia publications. Although this great advancement in transport was a financial boon to the merchant in reducing his staggering costs of shipping, the ultimate beneficiary was the consumer.*

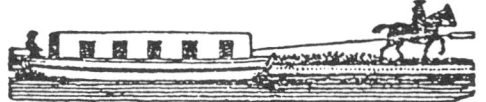

### BOATING AND FORWARDING.

### MONEY SAVED BY THE FARMER AND MERCHANT.

THE subscribers would most respectfully mention to the business portion of the community, that they have erected a large, convenient and safe Warehouse on the Chesapeake and Ohio Canal and Baltimore & Ohio Railroad, at Harpers Ferry, Va., at which place they will always be ready and willing to receive Merchandise, Grain, Flour, &c., for re-shipment either to the District of Columbia or Baltimore, or any points West of this place. They would state that they make their charges to correspond with the times. They have Boats constantly running from this point to the District of Columbia; and keep constantly on hand, during the season,

**Salt, Fish, Plaster, Lumber, &c.,**

which they will sell at the lowest market prices, and on fair terms.

HUNTER & DOWLING.
Harpers-Ferry, Oct. 16, 1849.

### APPOMATTOX RAIL ROAD.

CHANGE IN THE HOUR OF STARTING.

On and after Monday, the 4th Feb., the Mail and Passenger Trains will leave Petersburg On Mondays, Wednesdays and Fridays, at 7¾ o'clock, a. m., taking passengers to Steamer Mount Vernon.

INLAND ROUTE TO THE SOUTH, through Baltimore, Washington, Richmond, Petersburg, etc.—Travellers are informed that the railroads on this route are now finished into the interior of North Carolina.

GET THE
# Facts
ABOUT THE
SELF-STARTING SIX-CYLINDER
# Winton Six

Our page advertisements in current magazines tell some of them. Our catalog tells more. Write today.

48 H.P. 5 passenger car $3000
60 H.P. 7 passenger car $4500

**The Winton Motor Carriage Co.**
BEREA ROAD N.W., CLEVELAND, O., U.S.A.

# HOW A TYPICAL VIRGINIA COUNTRY STORE EVOLVED

1. A store from post-Colonial times was usually a bare bones building, often dark and poorly heated by a wood stove.

2. Merchants added a storage shed, front porch and perhaps a basement. Overhead storage areas often were abandoned.

3. About the mid-1850s, a second floor appeared as living quarters for the merchant and his family and later for his clerk. Often the center aisle was widened and tables were placed end to end in the aisle and loaded with merchandise. Large glass windows were added. Coal replaced wood for heating.

4. By the 1900s, some stores enlarged, expanding their lines of merchandise to include a greater variety of products, such as appliances, agricultural implements, automotive supplies, and fuel.

# SETTING UP SHOP

From post-Revolutionary days, the most popular country store building was a rectangle with a tall A-roof. On the front, above the entrance, was a large opening through which were hoisted the crates, boxes, and barrels of merchandise to be stored until needed. Some merchants later added a basement for exceptionally heavy items or perishables subject to weather extremes.

On the inside was a center aisle with counters on either side and shelves behind from floor to ceiling. Somewhere central to the inside was a wood burning stove.

Storekeepers developed many theories about merchandising, including where items should be placed for the best sales advantage. J. C. Penney considered it important enough to take a survey. He found that most men, upon entering a building, turned to the right, and most women turned to the left. Accordingly, he placed his women's line of merchandise on the left. Other merchants followed this pattern.

As storekeepers also became postmasters, differing opinions evolved concerning placement of the Post Office within the store. Some proprietors preferred to have the Post Office at the front, where postal customers would not interfere with store business. Others placed it at the rear of the store, convinced that people with postal business also would see merchandise they might need as they passed through.

Early country stores were fairly dark, having only a few windows and small ones at that. Glass was expensive and security was important. Small windows, shuttered and bolted from the inside, were difficult to break down.

By the mid-19th Century, stores began adding an upstairs living quarters for the owners, often also providing a room or rooms for the store clerk and extra storage space for seasonal items. Toward the end of the 19th Century, as glass in large sheets became available, the more prosperous stores had display windows added to the front of the building. A variety of items on display and increased light inside were always good for business.

Often store shelves would tower 10 to 12 feet off the floor. Arm extenders helped retrieve those items high up. Storekeepers also had rolling ladders installed along the fronts of shelves for easier access.

*The storekeeper's friend, an arm extender or shelf reacher in use. It enabled the merchant to greatly increase his shelf display area.*

Many a clerk impressed the young ladies with his dexterity by dislodging an item from a high shelf with an arm extender and deftly catching it with one hand, perhaps even behind his back.

Another distinctive feature of country

 *This is a fine example of a false-front country store. Recently modernized, this Albemarle County building is now home to a flourishing new business.*

stores during the later Victorian era was the false front or billboard front. It provided a large display area for signage, which some merchants found desirable. This architectural feature was used extensively on commercial buildings throughout the settlement of the West.

As store buildings increased in size, the center aisles expanded. Long tables were placed end to end down the aisle for the display of seasonal merchandise: seeds and garden tools in spring, fresh produce in summer and fall, and Christmas items later on. To display new and attractive merchandise usually kept customers returning more frequently to keep up with the times.

When coal became readily available, stores switched from wood for several reasons. In winter, a severe cold spell meant trouble for the merchant trying to keep his store warm through the night. A wood fire died before morning. A coal fire could be banked to last the night and proved to be cheaper.

The wooden crates that most items came packed in were very handy for kindling a stove fire. And, if you ever visited an old country store, you may have noted the circuitous route of stove pipe overhead used by the merchant to carry smoke to the outside. The shrewd shopkeeper gleaned all the heat he could from the pipe.

As community populations increased noticeably, a merchant with a Post Office soon had competition. If that merchant happened to be a Democrat, and the national political scene looked strongly favorable for a Republican presidential candidate, it was a safe bet that a would-be merchant with Republican credentials opened a rival store. Usually, he was well-assured of receiving the postmastership from the incoming Republican Administration. A Post Office greatly assisted the new storekeeper financially and brought in customers of his rival.

By the 1920s, good roads and automobiles had eliminated many smaller stores located near communities that were taking on city status. The small country merchant could not compete with prices or the variety offered by specialty stores or city merchants.

Country stores safely away from growing towns prospered. Many became dealers for nationally advertised products. Big ticket items, like home appliances, stoves and furnaces, automobile tires and accessories, and brand name agricultural implements, even tractors, became part of the merchant's line. Scores of country merchants lived quite comfortably, owned farms, and sent their children to college.

Then came Black Tuesday and the stock market collapse of 1929. In conversations with a number of shopkeepers, it surprised me to discover that most were not too seriously affected by the Depression. In the country, people cultivated gardens. They had pigs, chickens and eggs, perhaps a cow or goat for milk and butter, and raised a calf or two. In other words, country folk were generally self-sufficient and the barter system served them well. The Barter Theater (Virginia's State Theater) in Abingdon was born in this period of time.

In the aftermath of the stock market collapse, incoming President Franklin D. Roosevelt declared a national emergency in 1932 and closed the nation's banks for a short time. The government then issued "scrip" as a substitute for money to bring back confidence in and stability to the nation's economy.

One problem for shopkeepers at the time were the itinerants breaking into their stores for food or whatever of value they could carry. In one small town near the railroad, a merchant, who had also been mayor, told me that on extremely cold nights he would open up the town's jail, which was usually empty, and in the morning find two or three drifters asleep inside. The barred windows that remain on stores date to this period.

I came across the books and records of a country store built in 1913. The listing of gross sales from the 1920s to 1939 told a different story than I had been led to believe. The year 1927 was the high point, when sales reached $17,000. From 1930 on, income began to decline until 1937 when gross sales dropped below $6,000. The war in Europe and America's war preparedness helped the economy quickly recover and country stores again

*Many old store windows, like the one above, still retain the bars placed there to discourage burglaries. Stores located near railroad tracks were particularly vulnerable to break-ins.*

prospered. But in reality, that was the final flourish to the end of an era.

After World War II, manufacturing and merchandising dramatically changed the way retail businesses operated. Supermarkets and discount stores carried new and innovative products. Television advertising, plus slick, color magazine ads greatly enhanced consumer sales. Having money in their pockets for the first time since pre-Depression days, and having been deprived of many "necessities" through the five plus years of the war, the whole country went on a new product buying spree.

Try as he may, it was impossible for the rural merchant to compete with city stores. In remote areas, merchants held on for a while, but the handwriting was on the wall.

There were some merchants who remained open because their store was their life. Customers were friends and they couldn't give that up.

There were even isolated cases where stores were closed down and abandoned with items still on the shelves and in the storerooms. I came across one such store, but was never able to gain permission to enter. The windows were barred and smudged with dirt so that a view of the interior was impossible. This store was eventually torn down, so for me, the mystery remains.

Occasionally, I've come across store buildings while driving through rural areas. Usually they were old stores that had been converted to homes or apartments. In very remote areas, I've found stores empty and deteriorating, but their telltale architecture still conjured up memories of an era.

# CHAPTER 2  THE BUSINESS OF TENDING A GENERAL STORE

The work of an 18th and 19th Century merchant differed dramatically from that of a storekeeper in the 1930s. Merchandise was not packaged. The proprietor of an early store or his clerk, if he could afford one, had to scoop or count, weigh or measure, wrap and tie almost every item sold. Merchandise came in barrels and wooden crates. Farm produce was purchased by the wagon load.

The merchant had to have ample storage space for quantities of goods and staples. He also needed to keep an accurate tally of his inventory, noting when he was running low on certain stock or perhaps needed to push items because they were not selling, or even spoiling.

Buying seasonal produce was often a gamble for most early storekeepers.

Another vexing problem for the early merchant was money. Dealing with the many different coins and paper bills in circulation was very complicated because face values fluctuated from state to state and region to region. There were British shillings, and Spanish reales or bits (hence a quarter referred to as two bits), as well as Dutch and French coins. During the Revolution, our Continental Congress issued paper bills and coins as did each of the 13 colonies. After 1792, the United States Mint produced coins backed by the government.

From 1836 on, only state chartered banks were allowed to issue currency. During the Civil War, the federal government enacted the National Banking Act and issued paper money that became known as "greenbacks". From that time on, only money issued by the United States Government was legal tender.

This created losses for merchant and customer alike, but stabilized a chaotic monetary sys-

*Coins most familiar to early merchants included (a) a fippenny bit or 1/2 reale, Spanish, equal to 6 1/2 cents, (d) the 2 bits Spanish, worth approximately 25 cents, both from Mexico. U. S. coins are (c) a large copper penny and (b) a silver 50-cent piece. (Below) Early U. S. paper bills were called "Continentals".*

tem, except in the Confederate South.

Early merchants also used their own form of money known as "due bills". A receipt was given by the merchant to a farmer in payment for the produce brought to the store. If the merchant was of good standing in the community, the farmer could use this receipt or due bill to pay other debts or use it as credit for purchases from the merchant.

In reviewing merchants' books for the period between the Revolution and the Civil War, most bills were settled in trade. For example, a customer charged daily necessities for three months, then gave the merchant a load of firewood or produce. If that was not enough, he paid the balance in hard money.

The savvy merchant, through his astute attention to his customers' needs and preferences, became a community leader and general purveyor of knowledge and information.

In a real sense, he was a banker, carrying customers on credit and often extending credit through bad times. Merchants even maintained savings accounts for some customers. He was a commission agent, finding city markets for produce his customers raised. In times of emergency, he was a doctor, with his knowledge of patent medicines and home remedies learned from other customers. He was a veterinarian, since most farms experienced sick animals. He was a lawyer, giving opinions on personal matters, drawing up simple legal contracts or even a person's will.

Through the passage of time and the character traits and habits of the owner, a store developed a personality. It was something often sensed when walking through the door. Most were warm and orderly, congenial, occasionally dark and forbidding, but always exciting in the sense that whatever was happening, the storekeeper would know about it. The amount of stock on the shelves and the variety of products told a great deal about the store, the area it served, and the business acu-

 *During the Depression, merchants paid their local suppliers of produce with "due bills" (below). These store tokens are from Virginia stores closed many years ago.*

men of the proprietor.

There was one unwritten rule, perhaps commandment, endorsed by all merchants. Never allow a customer behind the counter! In fact, failure to observe this rule by a customer often resulted in a stern rebuke or in bodily harm.

Packaged and canned goods began appearing on merchant shelves in the 1860s and 1870s, but it remained a chore to scoop, weigh, bundle, and tie many products until the beginning of the 20th Century.

A large portion of the 18th and 19th Century storekeeper's merchandise had to be ordered and shipped to him from some major commercial center. This source of supply usually was decided long before he opened his store. To select his stock and place his order for the coming year, the merchant made an annual trip to the commercial center, canvassed the wholesale houses, and then purchased his stock. Afterward, he negotiated shipping arrangements with a reliable teamster or a railroad. Sometimes both were required for delivery of his goods.

In an 1890s book entitled *The Old Pike*, I discovered the following true story of crime and detection in which a merchant was victimized and turned sleuth to produce amazing results. Though not strictly a Virginia occurrence, it illustrates some of the difficulties encountered by early merchants. The gist of the story follows:*

*This is a scene on a busy early 19th Century turnpike as wagoneers put in for the night at a tavern.*

> During the early spring of the year 1823, an Ohio merchant named Boring took passage on a stagecoach for Baltimore to purchase a stock of fresh goods. West of Cumberland, two merchants named Keagy and Crider of Salisbury, Somerset County, Pennsylvania, took seats in the same coach, destined also for Baltimore on a like mission. It required considerable time to reach Baltimore, and the three merchants formed a strong friendly relationship.
>
> Reaching Baltimore, they stopped together at the same hotel and talked over their business, the quality and quantity of goods required by each forming the leading topic of their conversation. They went out among the wholesale stores of the city and bought the goods they desired.
>
> The stock purchased by Boring was decidedly larger, finer and more varied than the stock bought by the Somerset county merchants. Upon completing his purchases, Boring's first thought was to have his goods safely shipped upon the best terms obtainable.
>
> Keagy and Crider kindly offered their services to aid him in engaging a trusty wagoner to haul his goods to Ohio. They introduced one named Tissue as the right man for that purpose. Tissue was engaged, but he soon discovered one wagon bed would not hold all the goods.
>
> Tissue introduced another wagoner by the name of Mitchell, who was engaged to haul the remnant that could not be handled by Tissue. Boring, having

*The Old Pike, by T. B. Searight, published by author, 1894.

arranged for the transportation of his goods, said good-bye to his friends Keagy and Crider, and left for his home in Ohio.

His goods not arriving when due, he supposed some accident had caused a delay, and that they would be forthcoming as soon as practicable. But as days and weeks passed, Boring began to feel uneasy about the long delay. He wrote the consignors in Baltimore for an explanation. They replied that the goods had been carefully loaded on the wagons of Tissue and Mitchell, according to the agreement, and they knew nothing of their destiny beyond that.

Boring then took to the road to find his goods. He went first to Baltimore and learned that Tissue and Mitchell had left the city, with the goods in their wagons, and proceeded westward. He traced them as far as Hagerstown, Maryland, and at that point lost all trace of them.

He proceeded to Cumberland without tidings of his lost goods. From Cumberland he went on, making inquiry at every tavern and toll gate, until he reached Somerfield. Still he had heard nothing of Tissue or his companion, Mitchell. He put up for the night at a tavern in Somerfield, and while at supper discovered an important clue. The waiting maid at the table wore a tortoise shell comb, resembling very much those in a package he had bought in Baltimore. In polite and delicate terms, he inquired of the girl where she obtained so handsome a comb. She replied, "In a store at Salisbury."

In an instant, Boring recalled his fellow merchants and recent fellow travelers, Keagy and Crider, of Salisbury, but concluded that they had purchased the same quality of combs in Baltimore. He went to bed, intent upon continuing his research along the road, but during the night he changed his mind.

In the morning, Boring returned directly to Salisbury. Reaching Salisbury, he entered a store and, to his amazement, saw upon the counters and shelves various articles which he recognized as belonging to his stock.

After thoroughly satisfying himself that he had found his goods, Boring proceeded to Somerset and swore out a warrant.

Investigation disclosed a remarkable example of criminal conduct. Keagy, Crider, Tissue, and Mitchell had entered into a conspiracy to steal Boring's goods. The acquaintance formed on the stagecoach constituted the initial point of the scheme, and Keagy and Crider found ready confederates in Tissue and Mitchell. There was, of course, to be a division of the spoils.

To avoid identification, the wagoners changed the color of their wagon beds, and upon reaching Hagerstown diverged from the main road and took the country byways.

The goods were placed first in a large barn in the vicinity of Salisbury, and then carried in small lots to the store of Keagy & Company. A portion of the goods, consisting of fine chinaware thought to be too expensive for the Salisbury trade, was broken up and buried.

Keagy was first arrested and promptly gave bail for trial. Goaded by the weight of his offense, he soon thereafter committed suicide. Tissue and Crider fled the jurisdiction and were never apprehended. No mention was recorded of the other guilty wagoner.

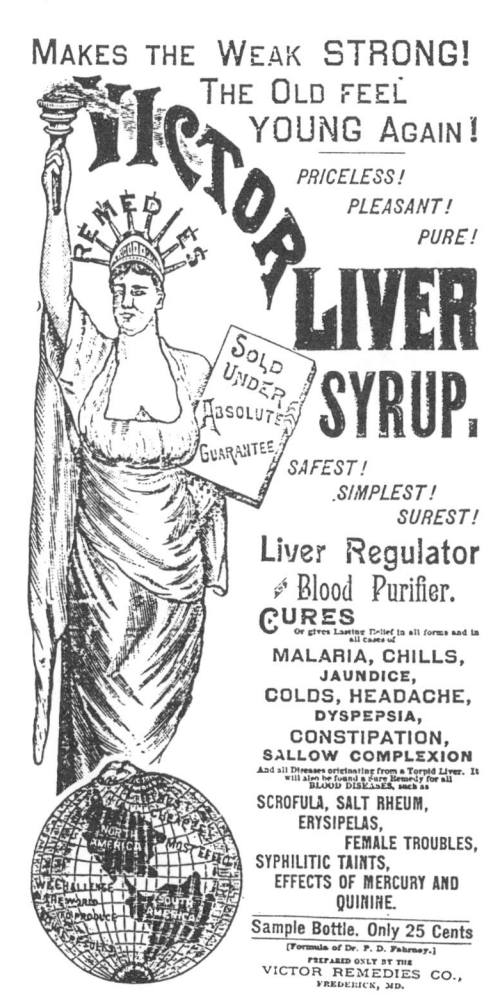

In this case the merchant was fortunate in being able to reclaim part of his goods. A loss of a year's stock could have meant bankruptcy.

By the end of the 1860s, newer wholesale houses began sending out salesmen, then referred to as "drummers", in hopes of taking trade from the large established commercial houses. This gave country merchants the opportunity to order without the hassle of an annual pilgrimage to the big city.

By 1900, the drummer or salesman on the road reigned supreme, allowing storekeepers to order merchandise monthly or even weekly as needed, no longer requiring storage of items for a whole year. And many of these wholesale houses also delivered.

During the period from the 1860s to the 1900s, more and more products came prepackaged. Patent medicines, tobacco products, and an endless variety of canned and preserved foods came on the market. All of this prepackaging greatly aided the shopkeeper, reducing the time spent and losses resulting from scooping, weighing, and wrapping loose or bulk products.

There were common misconceptions about patent medicines. Most contained varying amounts of alcohol. Often, it was the vehicle that helped compound the ingredients. Other manufacturers used alcohol as a placebo in patent medicines to help customers feel better quickly. But the most compelling reason to add alcohol was to keep the product from freezing in winter. Cases of bottles would sit in unheated warehouses, on boxcars and wagons, and even in the stores themselves where winter temperatures would drop dramatically overnight and ruin any unprotected product.

For the merchant, patent medicines and tobacco products usually gave him his highest markups and guaranteed repeat customers. Incidentally, the "patent" of a medicine referred only to the name, not the medicine or its formula.

For years, Lydia Pinkham's Compound for Women was both praised and ridiculed. Finally, in the 1940s, it was scientifically analyzed and found to contain estrogen, a hormone whose replacement has proven to be beneficial to women.* Through four generations, there was a Pinkham

*Lydia Pinkham Is Her Name, by Jean Burton, Farrar, Straus & Co., 1949

woman helping answer the thousands of inquiries received by the Pinkham Company.

Through national advertising, and before the pure food and drug laws were enacted, many wild and unsubstantiated claims were quoted on behalf of scores of medicines, and made quite a few entrepreneurs rich and famous.

On one occasion, recorded years later, a wealthy medicine manufacturer brought a business acquaintance to his country estate. Along the way the guest inquired, "Does your medicine really work?" Stopping his fashionable rig on a high point overlooking his vast estate, the manufacturer waved his arm with a flourish and replied, "Well, you can see what it has done for me!"

## KEEPING THE BOOKS

The pulse of any country store was recorded and maintained in its books. At first, record keeping may have been haphazard with some shopkeepers, but they soon learned the importance of accurate bookkeeping. Jotting down every transaction, regardless of how small, became automatic to a good merchant. Most followed the system of keeping a daily sheet, which was transferred to a bound ledger at the end of the day or perhaps at the week's end. A single entry ledger was preferred by most, but the double entry system was used by merchants with larger inventories.

Another practice enjoyed for a while was the personal book. A small bound book was provided to each customer. Whenever the customer or family member came to the store for a purchase, it was recorded in the personal book as well as the store book. That way, the customer was certain that no "accidental" listing of merchandise would be found on his bill.

The ultimate system for storekeepers was manufactured by the McCaskey Company in Alliance, Ohio. It was a large wooden cabinet encasing metal pages hinged at the back, forming a large book or file cabinet. Each page had spring clips of a size to hold small receipts. The merchant was supplied with small receipt pads with carbon pages. When a charged sale was made, a receipt was written with a carbon copy. The copy went to the customer and the original went in the spring clip file. At the end of a week or month, the file of receipts was totaled for the customer, who used his carbon copies to easily confirm the amount recorded by the merchant.

About the turn of the century, a new invention for storekeepers was sweeping the cities. It was the cash register. One of the benefits offered to store owners was keeping the clerks honest by printing an exact record of the sales.

Frankly, in my early store visits, I never encountered more than two or three cash registers. Most merchants were satisfied with the cash drawer method of keeping money. A cash drawer was suspended under the counter and out of sight for safekeeping. Most had a bell that gonged when the drawer was opened. There also were finger tabs in the drawer pull. Of the four or five tabs, the correct two, set by the merchant, had to be depressed to allow the drawer to open. This was another safety feature that could baffle a would-be thief from reaching over the counter for the drawer when the merchant was occupied elsewhere. In the drawer were hollowed-out compartments for coins and rectangles for bills. Simple, but effective.

*Merchant's cash drawer.*

I have heard and read complaints about the stores being cluttered, dark and dirty, with people tripping over items displayed on the floor

and stacked in front of the counters. Granted, there were untidy merchants. But for the most part, they put out their merchandise to be seen. If you accidentally tripped on something, you weren't paying proper attention to the storekeeper's wares. Or perhaps, tripping brought your attention to a particular item.

Another aspect of merchandising religiously adhered to was never, ever leave a shelf space empty. Storekeepers always had as many articles out on display as possible.

Almost all store owners were honest and reliable, but there persisted a tale about the merchant who had "sold his thumb a thousand times" by slightly depressing the scales in his favor. Then there was the story of a merchant who had sent his son to college by adding a penny or so to the "tick" or bill of his customers over many years.

Conversely, there were stories about customers putting one over on the storekeeper. One concerned a merchant who kept in his front store window a pre-printed sign with changeable numbers that told his customers what he was paying for eggs and butter that week. Two young farm lads decided to play a little trick on the merchant. Waiting for the morning when the merchant went to town to do his banking, the lads entered the store. One engaged the daughter minding the store in lengthy conversation, while the other went quietly to the store window and changed the sign's prices upward to the selling price. Then both lads left.

As word quickly spread through the neighborhood, the daughter unknowingly enjoyed a small rush of trade in eggs and butter. The jokesters were far away before the merchant returned.

*(Left) Here is an interior view of an old country store still operating in the 1960s. (Above) Note the country merchant's crowded rolltop desk with his cat warming his chair.*

## FROM WRAP & TIE TO BAGS

The era of paper bags was a long time in coming, partly because the era of cheap paper was a long time in coming. It wasn't until after the Civil War that inexpensive paper came on the market.

Up until 1800, all paper was made by hand labor and was fairly costly and in short supply. A practical paper-making machine was invented in the early 1800s, but since this process depended upon rags of cotton fiber, the same raw material used in handmade paper, the supply was not increased.

After the Civil War, several methods of making paper from wood pulp were introduced. These early processes produced new paper sources at cheaper prices. In the 1870s, paper bags became popular, with unlimited supplies in a great variety of sizes. Then, along with paper bags, came cardboard and corrugated boxes to replace the crates.

## WEIGHTS & MEASURES

Merchants could not do business without scales. They appeared in many sizes and shapes. There was not a commodity in existence for which a storekeeper didn't have a scale.

The oldest form was the balance scale with its assorted weights. Spring scales became popular, but their accuracy was often questionable. In fact, after the 1900s, many states enacted laws banning spring scales and establishing a regular inspection of commercial scales to insure uniformity to national standards.

Other indispensable objects for keeping store were the measures for liquids and dry produce. There were tin containers equal to one gill (four gills to a pint), one pint, one quart, one half-gallon, and one gallon. Barrels held from 31 to 42 gallons, depending on the liquid.

Any astute merchant usually had the following committed to memory.

Dry measure: two pints to a quart, eight quarts to a peck, four pecks to a bushel, 36 bushels to a chaldron.

Dry measure for barrels: flour was 196 pounds; beef, pork or fish were 200 pounds.

Dry weight for produce by the bushel: onions, 57 pounds; dried apples or peaches, 28 pounds; wheat, beans, peas or potatoes, 60 pounds.

A sack of wool was 308 pounds, a bale of cotton was 400 pounds, while a firkin of butter was either 50 or 100 pounds, and a pack of wool equalled 240 pounds, the pack load for a horse.

# A VARIETY OF MERCHANT SCALES

*Illustrated are: (1) A scale beam, (2) a steelyard, (3) a platform scale, (4) different forms of spring scales, (5) countertop scales.*

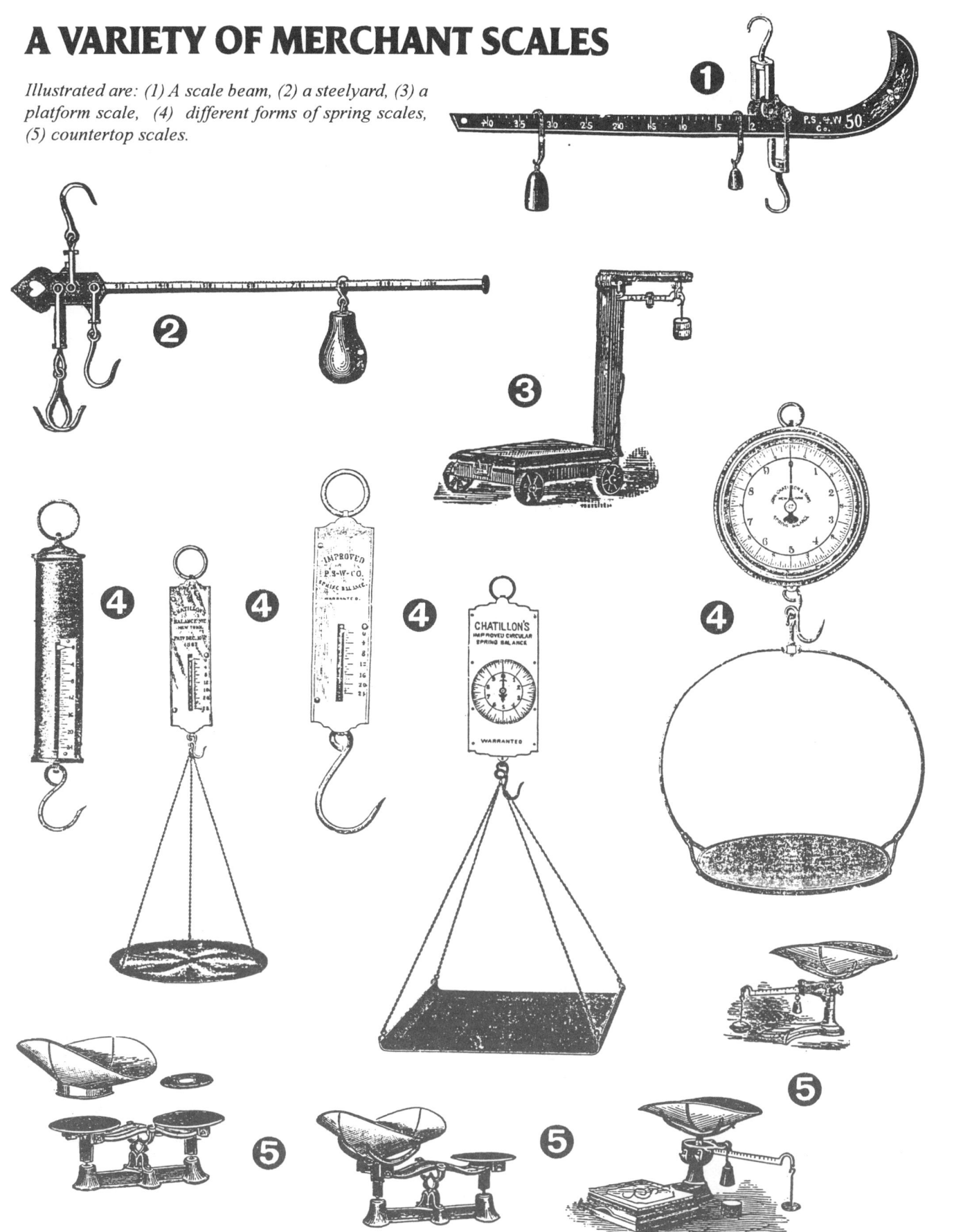

## OTHER STORE NECESSITIES

Near the end of the Civil War, an increase in the sheet glass supply found a ready market with makers of display cases for stores. Though quite expensive and ornate, the early cases were eagerly purchased by city merchants who had large inventories. Most cases were built to fit on top of existing counters. But as styles and customs changed, display cases were fashioned to be glass from the floor up to counter height. With the changing styles in city stores came used showcases. Enterprising salesmen were on the lookout for these items and secured them for their country merchants at bargain prices.

Some of the most useful and attractive cases were the curved glass or "waterfall" front cases. Items displayed in them, especially candy, gave the illusion of being touchable. The observant merchant was certain to wipe off finger and nose prints left by young customers during the day.

There were other fixtures that caught the eye. Until the era of vacuum packaged coffee in the 1930s, you always found a large, ornately decorated red coffee grinder prominent on a counter in the store.

In early stores, merchants roasted their own coffee beans. Then came preroasted beans and all the merchants had to do was grind them. That in itself was work. To grind 10 pounds of beans took time and muscle. But the aroma of ground coffee throughout the store was surpassed only by the smell of fresh-baked bread.

One other item that was certain to be found on a convenient counter was the "wheel" of cheese. Many stores had a special device for cutting wedges from rounds of cheese. It was a flat circular platform slightly larger than the cheese that was placed upon it. A tall, thin, sharp blade attached to a moving arm rotated around the edges and across the metal platform. Storekeepers became expert at cutting a cheese wedge of any size.

These golden wheels of cheddar or "rat" cheese were popular with customers and a mer-

*(Top) This is the most picturesque form of a store coffee grinder. They came in a variety of sizes and shapes. (Below) Here is a device for measuring and cutting wedges from a "wheel" of cheese.*

chant with a good run of trade sold 10 to 15 wheels a year. Those good cheddars left a pungent aroma often detected when first walking into the store.

A country merchant within a prosperous community found another way to keep his male customers away from the city stores. Clothiers in the large trade centers, like Baltimore, prepared giant sales catalogues, usually measuring about two feet by two feet. They contained pictures of the latest men's fashions in the front, followed by cut squares of material samples pasted onto the pages. The most important parts were the instruction sheet for the merchant on exactly how to measure a man for a suit, and an order form with blanks for the measurements. With this detailed sheet and the number from the material sample included, the store's order was mailed off. In a matter of weeks, the "hand tailored" suit arrived for the anxiously waiting customer.

Every year a new catalogue with current styles was prepared to replace the old one. Yet in visiting these stores, I didn't come across any old style books with the material samples still in place. A storekeeper finally solved the little mystery for me. "Oh, my wife takes those for her quilting," he said.

Kerosene lamps were the main source of artificial light available to stores in the country. By the 1900s, a store near a community that had a small electric plant may have been fortunate enough to have electricity. Most stores had to wait for the Rural Electrification Administration (R.E.A.) in the 1930s to bring them electricity.

The telephone also was a late convenience to help the country store. The biggest benefits the phone offered a storekeeper were in ordering a necessary item quickly for a favored customer and having a means of communication in case of an emergency.

I encountered one store that had been on the border between two small telephone companies. For the sake of his customers, the merchant had one telephone from each system installed side-by-side in his store. This enabled customers in one area to communicate with friends in the other through a three-way conversation with an accommodating merchant.

In one mountainous region of Central Virginia, I came to a very large, but almost empty, store which at one time must have held an impressive array of merchandise. "Yes," said the shopkeeper, "this store once kept two clerks busy!" He went on to explain that in earlier times a turnpike had passed by the store, crossing the nearby mountains and bringing trade from miles around. In the late fall, the giant storage area was filled with smoked hams and produce. Outside were pens of fine turkeys and geese, brought in by the mountain people. Before the holidays, buyers from as far away as Richmond and Baltimore arrived to order for their commercial houses. Such was the reputation of this store and its stock in trade. Then the government came along, bought up all the mountain land to make a national park, and scattered the suppliers to the wind. Next, the turnpike across the mountains was relocated and all the traffic was diverted elsewhere.

And speaking of location, another remarkable incident was told to me by a country mer-

*This fine old store building in Madison County had such a run of trade it once required the assistance of two store clerks.*

chant. His father kept store at a place he came to believe was not as prosperous or advantageous as it should be. Finding a better situation several miles away, he arranged with local teamsters to move his store on log rollers to the new site. During the move he did business as usual, never once closing his doors.

I have always wondered how the storekeeper managed to keep his merchandise on the shelves.

That story reminded me that when farmers wanted to get their livestock to market in the days before trucks, many had "drives" the same as in the Old West but for much shorter distances.

One storekeeper, who dealt in turkeys, told me about a farmer who drove his turkeys several miles to the storekeeper's pens. Turkeys, not noted for their great intelligence, required quite a few hands and some steady nerves as hundreds were driven along a public road. Luckily, there was only horse and buggy traffic and very little of that.

Each hand carried a long pole which was used constantly to flush the turkeys out of trees along the way and guide any wandering fouls in the desired direction.

Another merchant, whose store was in a small town at the foot of the mountains, remembered there was a valley nearby where area farmers sent their beef cattle in spring. They drove the cattle right through town out to the valley to graze all summer. Then the hands went to the bar at the old hotel and the town was jumping for a day or so. Late in fall, the hands returned and drove the cattle home.

Another community also felt the effects of the federal government and its acquisition of mountain land. As I drove down the main street of

*A sheep drive is winding its unhurried way down a country road to market.*

this small town, I counted at least three empty store buildings on one side and possibly two on the other. Intrigued, I finally came across an old-time resident who told me the following story:

"Back in the 1930s, when the government bought up the (nearby) mountain land, they moved out all the people that had lived in those mountains for many generations. Having no place to go, some settled here. And for the first time in their lives they had money, lots of money, from the government buying up their land.

"They began drinking and carousing and disturbing the town, acting so badly that to be rid of them, the merchants just closed up shop and left."

The last time I went through, two of the old buildings had been torn down and a three-story building had been reduced to two.

Somewhere in a general store, on the end of a counter, was a paper dispenser with a roll of brown paper firmly in place behind the cutter bar. If there was a butcher's counter, it had a roll of white paper. Wholesale houses often had brand names and trademarks printed continuously on the paper rolls for additional free advertising. If a particular store was a favored customer, the wholesaler printed the merchant's store name and location under the trademark.

Once, in the back room of a country store, I found a large unused roll of wrapping paper with an emblem of a product long gone from the market. In answer to my query the merchant explained, "My father refused to use it because the printer had misspelled the name of our location." Pride came before thrift.

In an occasional store, I was given the privilege of visiting the merchant's store room. Here were kept the myriad tools and devices required for dealing with the variety of cartons and containers of merchandise.

There were crow bars for prying tops from barrels and wooden crates, bung borers and spigots for barrels of liquids, heavy metal ice tongs and ice picks, tenterhooks for hanging meats and poultry, numerous sizes of scoops, pails and buckets, and a variety of tins for measuring out liquids.

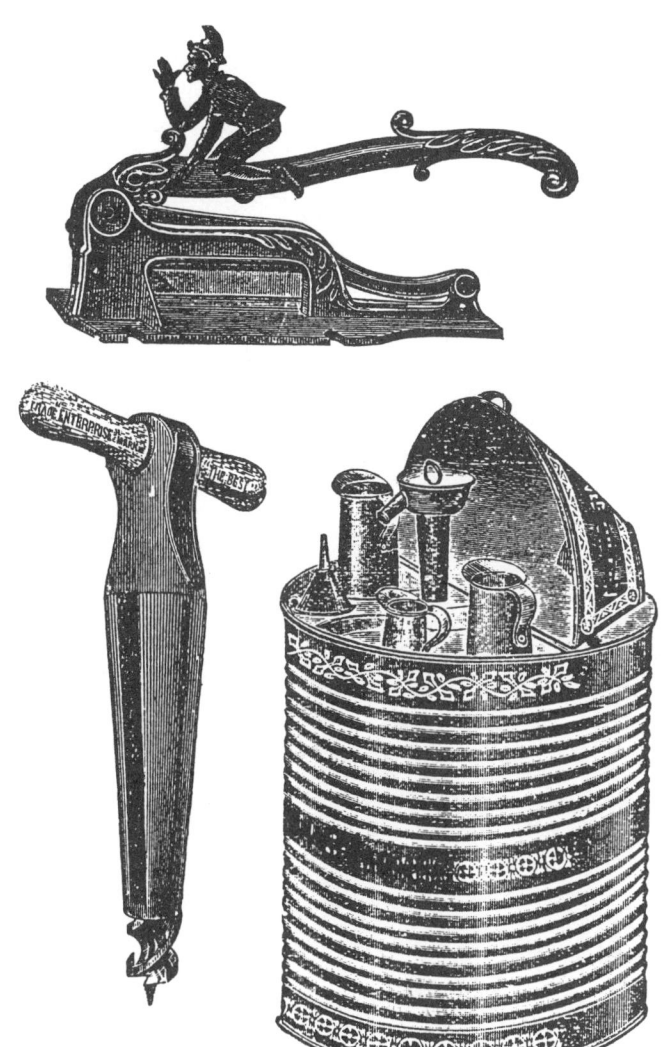

*(Top) Chewing tobacco in earlier times came to the merchant in long hard strips. With this device he would slice off an inch or two of tobacco for the customer. (Left) This is a bung starter used to bore a hole in the end of a wooden barrel holding liquid. A spigot was then inserted to withdraw its contents. (Above) An early container for storing and dispensing kerosene, this is called a "Baltimore oil tank".*

By the 1960s, these implements lay idle, no longer necessary for the country storekeeper. Of course, a few still measured out kerosene from a 55-gallon drum, but that was about the only item sold from bulk.

The final generation of country merchants quietly passed on. But perhaps one of the salesmen in *The Music Man* said it best: "Who's gonna patronize a little-bitty two-by-four kinda store anymore?"

*A gathering of neighbors on the porch of this pre-Civil War country store in Louisa County.*

# CHAPTER 3  THE LIGHTER SIDE OF STOREKEEPING

For many years, in most of rural Virginia the ebb and flow of life centered around the country store. It was the repository of local lore and information, particularly so if the store also was the Post Office.

Here was the home away from home for the older male members of the community, especially in winter. Conversations ranged from crops and weather, hunting and fishing, who played what practical joke on whom, to medicines and who was sick, dying or dead. And, there was always politics.

Naturally, the country store became the center of attention for anyone seeking political office. Here was found the community elders and often the opinion formers. And, if the office seeker was an astute listener, he gained some valued insights as to the will of the people on issues of which he was perhaps unaware.

The comings and goings of community members often were observed by the merchant and his wife or clerk. It wasn't being nosy, exactly, it was just a way of life.

"Have you seen Hiram?" inquired a customer.

"Yes, he passed here about 7 o'clock this morning, probably on his way to help his brother Zeke with the haying," replied the storekeeper.

"Well, I guess I won't find him home 'till after supper then," returned the customer.

"There goes Doc Horsely," noticed the clerk, "probably up to the Aylor's place. Heard there was sickness there."

It was a way of neighbor keeping track of

neighbor. In times of trouble or a disaster, such as a fire, the store was a meeting place for planning a course of action and for gathering resources to help the victims. I found an interesting example of this in the Madison County Eagle newspaper of 1921.

"A strange animal had been seen on Courthouse Mountain and it had only been noticed at night so those who had seen it could not give a very accurate description of the creature. Then two brothers were out making the rounds of their rabbit traps when one brother was confronted by the animal. He said it appeared in front of him by a fence. It looked to be about 3 feet tall and was light brown in color except for the head which was covered with a shock of black hair. Seeing the lads, it reared up, gritting its teeth, and making a ferocious growl.

Both boys lost no time in getting out of there and have not been back to their traps since.

Another disturbance occurred one night at a house near the mountain. Something aroused turkeys roosting in a nearby tree. The dogs were sent to investigate but refused to follow the scent!

A party was being formed in Mr. _____'s store Saturday night to go out on Courthouse Mountain and look for the animal, but someone started telling ghost stories and this spoiled the expedition. Instead, the patrons went home in parties of two or more with the exception of Mr. _____ who really did venture to home by himself!"

The coming of radio changed forever how news was disseminated. Until the 1920s, most news arrived at the Post Office/country store via city newspapers and the drummers.

Somewhere in those establishments, in a conspicuous place, was a board for public notices and wanted posters from the police or the "G-men". With radio came news focusing attention on Prohibition and the crime wave sweeping the nation, caused in part by Prohibition. Bulletin boards were plastered with wanted posters reinforcing the news broadcasts.

On several occasions I came across government posters, still in place, warning storekeepers about customers buying excess amounts of sugar. It listed quantities likely to be sought that would indicate such a person was operating a still and should be reported to the authorities.

There was always time for fun and games at the country store. Often, there was a barrel placed near the stove convenient for a game of checkers. One store owner told me he might have two or three games of checkers going at one time in bad weather.

"But that was many years ago," he said. "The young ones don't play checkers any more."

*Long before the appearance of the penny scales in town and city stores, the country merchant was weighing the neighborhood children on his platform scales.*

 *This waterfall front showcase, with its tantalizing display of candies, is protected from "too close" human encounters by the thin iron railing that surrounds it.*

About five minutes later a young man entered the store. The proprietor interrupted our conversation to wait on the new arrival.

"Pardon me, but would you happen to have a checkers game for sale?" inquired the young man. With a heavy heart, the merchant confessed that he did not.

I've never been back to see if the storekeeper ordered a new supply of checkers.

In several stores, I found iron bars braced across the front of prominent showcases. In answer to my question, one storekeeper said that the frolicking occasionally got out of control and the bars prevented customers from falling into and breaking the showcases. With my curiosity aroused, I asked what kind of games or entertainment went on.

"The young'uns, wantin' to show how strong they was, would put a round cheesebox lid on the floor, shoulder a 200-pound sack o' meal and then try to jump into that lid and then jump out again," the store keeper related.

Sounded like an interesting challenge for Olympic competition.

Another fascinating bit of sport was told me by a different shopkeeper. He said there was a short but powerful bald-headed fellow who came around one day to take bets.

"Told me to get an empty ammo box, one of those sturdy finger jointed ones that had held shot gun shells, hold it against the counter and he would bet all takers that he could smash it to kindling with one blow of his head. After a few skeptics among the bystanders made a wager, I held the box up against the front of my counter, like he said. He walked back a ways, bent down, lowered his head and commenced running toward the box. Well, by gosh, his ole bald head hit that box and broke it all to smithereens. He collected his winnins, bought a soda and went on his way with no sign of any harm done him."

Many of the stores built before World

War I sold whiskey, usually in bottles. Only one store I discovered actually had a bar or tap room. That store dated to the 1850s, and the proprietor showed me a small room at the back of the store. It was dark with a high, dark wood counter and no seats or stools were visible. Space was so limited it couldn't have held more than six or seven customers at a time. But then, in such a remote rural area, the tap room doubtfully enjoyed that many customers at one time during its entire existence.

I'd heard stories of shopkeepers who were also barbers, but I was only able to locate one merchant who could give a shave and a haircut (but not for two bits). His barber's chair was on wheels and, when not in use, was pushed back out of the way. Now, I wish I had a photograph of the haircut I received.

Merchants aided the smaller communities in ways that showed a sincere concern for their neighbors. In one instance, a rural county had just put up a new school building and hired a teacher, but didn't have money in the budget for books. The nearby merchant, hearing of the problem, ordered the necessary books himself, and decided he would wait for payment if and when the funds were available.

Another storekeeper in a rural district undertook to supply the small school nearby with coal to make certain the children were kept warm.

I've heard of countless examples of merchants' generosity to their neighbors, as well as to strangers in troubled circumstances, often above and beyond the call of business.

An amusing yarn was passed on to me by the octogenarian mayor of a quiet Virginia town.

It seems a merchant with a large store adjacent to the railroad tracks enjoyed a prosperous run of trade. But on occasion, he made unwise business purchases, and one finally proved to be his undoing.

Previously, a salesman had convinced him to purchase a train car load of slat-bottom chairs. After a period of time, the merchant succeeded in selling enough chairs to clear his original investment. Encouraged by this first carload venture, he again succumbed to the golden oratory of another salesman and signed for a train car load of ceramic commodes. (This was the indispensable "necessary" that was kept under the bed before indoor plumbing.) In all probability, the items were at a bargain price because town water and sewer systems were making outhouses obsolete.

As time passed and the large inventory remained unsold, the merchant found himself

*An in-town store of Albemarle County, it once enjoyed a large run of trade.*

with a huge deficit and was forced into bankruptcy.

The auditors came in and pored over his books and papers. After an agonizing period of whispered activity and the shuffling of paper, the head auditor came to the merchant and said, "We have listed your liabilities, now where are your assets?"

"Follow me," replied the merchant, as he led the way to his large storehouse. "There," he said with a wave of his hand, "there are my assets!"

Before them stretched row upon row of stacked ceramic commodes.

After World War I, as more and more automobiles took to the roads, gasoline pumps began appearing at country stores across the state and nation. The pump most often seen was a metal cylinder about 16 feet tall. On the upper part was a glass reservoir with notches or rings to measure gasoline gallon by gallon. To activate the pump, a tall shaft attached to the base was worked backward and forward by hand. This sent gasoline up into the glass bowl at the top, the amount measured on the notches or rings. At the bottom of the glass bowl hung a hose which delivered gasoline from the bowl to a customer's automobile tank.

On one occasion, a customer pulled his car up to the pump, went inside, and told the storekeeper to "fill 'er up."

Out went the merchant, who pumped up what he judged was the amount of gasoline required to fill the tank. Once the glass reservoir held the correct amount, the storekeeper put the hose nozzle in the customer's gas tank, and with his eyes glued to the notches on the bowl, let the gas flow.

The level in the glass bowl kept dropping. Suddenly, as the automobile's owner watched, gas began spreading over the hood, down the side, along the running board, then dripping onto the ground.

The owner ran out shouting, "Henry, Henry, h'it's a-runnin' over!" The storekeeper shifted his gaze downward to the spreading gaso-

*This country store, like many others in the 1920s, began to capitalize on the prosperous trade to be derived from automobiles. They extended the roof to cover the newly installed gasoline pumps. Note the term "Filling Station".*

line, which by now had even begun soaking his pants legs. Bewildered, he looked back at the glass bowl markings then looked at his customer and said "Well, then, h'it ain't readin' right!"

A serious incident that occurred in one country store ended with an almost comical conclusion. One afternoon in summer, an automobile with three or four young men pulled up in front of a crossroads country store far removed from any large community. The store was run by a husband and wife. The husband noticed the auto's license plate was from out of state. As several youngsters wandered rather aimlessly around the store, the couple became suspicious of their intentions. Quietly, the wife removed most of the bills from the cash drawer and hid them under the counter. Within a short time, one youngster pulled out a pistol and demanded their money. The wife opened the drawer and they helped themselves to the contents and left, picking up a few food items on the way. As soon as the car was gone the merchant called the sheriff's office.

"Which route did they take?" the deputy asked.

As the merchant repeated the route number, both he and the voice on the phone gave a little chuckle. The route selected for the getaway dead-ended about five or so miles away.

"We'll come to the store and just wait nearby," said the deputy.

* * *

One evening, the word came that we had been expecting for some time. The old store, our friend and neighbor for a number of years, was closing.

The final day came and went. No mourners lingered about, and no band played a final dirge. It was a quiet passing.

That evening, as twilight approached, I walked down for one last glimpse of our departing friend. I stood in silent awe as my mind brought up visions of horses and wagons that pulled up to the store and were hitched to the rail in front. The brand names on the sacks of flour and chicken feed were almost legible as a clerk loaded them on a wagon. From inside came the soft orange glow of kerosene lanterns being lighted about the store. Tall shelves crammed with merchandise became visible through the glass front windows. But soon I heard the clatter of hooves as customers hurriedly drove their wagons to reach home before dark. As the last light of day faded to black, the country store disappeared. Forever.

 *A front-end loader methodically reduces to kindling this 100-year-old store building of Augusta County.*

# OLD VIRGINIA STORES
# A PICTURE ALBUM

*The following is a pictorial selection of store buildings I've collected from around the Old Dominion. They range in age from the 1750s to the 1930s. The categories are hopefully informative. The pictures illustrate the wide range of architectural variations to be found in Virginia. Most would be classified as examples of indigenous architecture--purely home-grown. Perhaps that is what we have come to love about them.*

*I have been saddened, as have many others, by the demise of numerous fine old mercantile businesses and buildings over the past decades. There are a few general stores still in business, I recently discovered. They are, however, only scaled-down versions of the store of old.*

*The real country general stores are alive in memories only, and those, too, are fading fast. Here are recorded some of the buildings that survive, before they become memories.*

*An old country store on the border of Prince George and Sussex counties returns to nature.*

# CLASSIC STORE BUILDINGS

This handsome brick structure sits in the midst of a very small community in Rockingham County. No longer open to the public, it served not only as a store and Post Office, but also as a courthouse and a meeting hall for social functions.

*(Above) Jackson's Store at Lahore in Orange County first opened in the very early 1800s and served customers until 1976. The building is an excellent example of early country store architecture.*

*(Below) The General Store in Buena Vista is a fine late 19th Century in-town store still in operation. Here may be found authentic and useful products of the past still manufactured and marketed today.*

 *In the quiet mountain community of McDowell stands this classic mid-19th Century store building. Currently, it is open to the public as an antique and gift shop, featuring homemade maple syrup.*

*This store (above) dates to the 1840s. Though no longer a country store, this handsome brick structure is still home to a flourishing business in Luray. The building (below) is an old store in new trappings.*

*It is always refreshing to see these once prosperous, but declining, old store buildings refurbished and still serving customers. This store is at the rural crossroads community of Wolftown, Madison County.*

*This country store (left) in Prince Edward County is a typical late 18th-early 19th Century building.*

*An old building (below) dating to the early 1800s, this perhaps best typifies a rural country store still open for business. Having survived a succession of merchants, this Wythe County store is a humble time machine. The past clings to the interior like wallpaper. Inside there persists the feeling that you could meet face-to-face with an ancestor.*

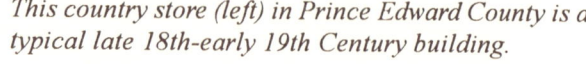

*This brick store structure (above right) of the 1840s is an addition to a much older log building. It is now preserved and serves as an antique shop at Mount Sidney in the Shenandoah Valley.*

*The brick building (below) was built in the 1830s as a guest house. It became a store in later years. Now an antique shop, it stands in the charming old community of Brownsburg in western Rockbridge County.*

*The fine frame building (top left) is a restored country store, again open for business in Snickersville, Loudoun County.*

*The store (bottom left) is one of the few mansard roofed store buildings to be found in rural Virginia. It now belongs to the Waterford Foundation of Loudoun County.*

*Here are three rare examples of Victorian false front facades located in the state. (Below) A store in Abingdon is open as a gourmet food shop and restaurant. The building (right) is an in-town store in Botetourt County, while the delightful building (bottom right) is in a rural area of Montgomery County.*

*The building, (above) the owner stated, incorporated a structure built in the late 1600s, which served as a trading post for early colonists. It stands at Dunnsville in Essex County.*

*Rector's General Store (below) of Atoka, in Loudoun County, first opened in 1842 and still is providing customers with a line of general merchandise.*

# THE STEPPED GABLE

*This interesting architectural feature was brought to America by colonists from Europe, predominantly by the Dutch. A typical example is the store (below) found in Scottsville, Albemarle County. The ever-innovative merchants decided this feature was more advantageous on the front of stores, often providing space for signage. The brick structure (right) is in Washington County.*

*Here are two interesting examples of stepped gable store front buildings (above) in Rockbridge County and (below) in Augusta County.*

*The country store (right) in Campbell County has been serving customers since the 1840s. Changes to the interior have been made through the years, but the flavor of the original store has been well maintained.*

*The spacious store building (below) once enjoyed a large run of trade. An early electric appliance sign is visible above the main door. Still hale and hearty, this building, at a major highway intersection in Greene County, now houses antique dealers.*

*Here is an empty store building on the Meadows of Dan in southern Virginia (above).*

*As with many former country store buildings, the one pictured (below) in the town of Surry still enjoys a good run of trade, but now in automobile parts and supplies.*

*Brick store buildings (above) in Rockbridge County and (below) in Fluvanna County sit quietly awaiting their fate.*

This diminutive store building (left) would eas[ily] qualify for a "smallest store" prize in this book. It w[as] an in-town store of Buckingham County.

This trim little store (below) is located in the town [of] Surry.

*A retired merchant purchased this old store (above) in Augusta County and converted it to a family gathering place.*

*This once-flourishing country store (below) in King William County sits by a busy highway, as a humble reminder of the changing times.*

# THE FALSE FRONT

 *The false-front store, though not as common as you might expect in Virginia, was found in great numbers throughout settlements in the West. Pictured here are examples from the counties of (1) Albemarle, (2) Culpeper, (3) Highland, and (4) Louisa.*

*In the Augusta County town of Middlebrook sits this general store (above) still in operation. Though modern on the inside, the exterior still informs the public of its past.*

*This quaint store building (below) once served customers in Appomattox County.*

# THE TWO-TIERED PORCH

*...ese country store buildings are easily adapted to ...rchandising items of the past. The store (right) in ...ederick County offers mementos of the Civil War.*

*...is large old country store (below) has been an an-...ue shop for many years. It is located on a major ...hway in Rockbridge County.*

[Th]is solid old store building (left) in Albemarle County [so]lemnly awaits a new proprietor and better times. [(B]elow left) With an upper tier extending over several [st]ops, this interesting store building of Rockingham [Co]unty now houses an antique shop, complete with [ca]rousel horse on the porch. (Right) Abandoned now [to] time and the elements, this store of Albemarle [Co]unty speaks of better days. (Bottom) The dark con[cre]te island that once held gas pumps (bottom right) [re]mains the only clue telling the curious that this at[tra]ctive building was once a general store. This, too, [is] in Albemarle County.

*The two empty store buildings (left) of Bedford County and (right) of Augusta County, depict the slow demise of most Virginia country stores.*

*Built in 1929 before the crash, this general store of Page County, situated near the Shenandoah River, has thrived over the years and remains in business today.*

In a remote section of Albemarle County, this delightfully Victorian country store, (right) though no longer in businesss, now houses descendants of the original merchant.

Nestled at the foot of a mountain in Highland County, (below) this store with Post Office continues to serve the public.

## WITH RESIDENCE ATTACHED

There were, no doubt, many favorable reasons why these merchants chose to live where they worked. In earlier times, they would have added living quarters above the store, but here they have either attached the store to their home or vice versa. The examples are (above) in Essex County, (below) Nelson County, (top right) Orange County, and (bottom right) Rockingham County.

59

This building in Essex County illustrates how a merchant converted a downstairs portion of this residence into a store. (Below) This is a country store and residence at Fort Mitchell deep in Lunenburg County. (Bottom) This scene depicts the store's mobile alarm system.

This interesting general store (right) in Roanoke County dates to the middle 1800s. It provides antique lovers with many fine rooms of period furniture for sale. The combined residence and country store (below right) in Louisa County offer a pleasant combination of differing architectural styles.

# IN-TOWN STORES

The in-town general store is, for the most part, quite different in appearance from a rural store. Town lots often dictated the proportions of most store buildings, giving them the look of a rectangular box. Pictured here are a variety of general stores from both large and small Virginia towns.

In the sketch (below) four of the five buildings visible were country stores at one time or another. Since the sketch was made, one store building has been torn down and the others greatly altered. None are open. This small community is in Orange County.

(Opposite right) Pictured here is an 1890s woodcut of a store in Staunton. (Far right) A large brick store building in Southampton County, (bottom right) the original portion of this brick building predates the Civil War. A large addition followed years later. Classes for the nearby college were first held in the 1880s on the store's upper floor. It is located in Bridgewater.

*Closed for many years, this store (left) of Shenandoah County has what appears to be a twin (opposite right). This building, originally built as a company store, has housed a number of merchants. Also in Shenandoah County, it still serves customers of the area.*

*A Post Office and a furniture store are still housed in this impressive structure serving the community of Draper in Pulaski County.*

*How clean and simple are the lines of this Augusta County structure, (below) which once housed a general merchant and an undertaker.*

Three of the four in-town store buildings pictured here do follow the rectangular box plan of many in-town stores. The one interesting exception (below) was seen on a major thoroughfare in Frederick County. Also shown (left) a store building in Dayton. Fronting on a railroad track in a residential area of Staunton (right opposite) sits this 100 year old store. It remains open to the public and displays mementos of the past above the shelves of modern day groceries, and (opposite below) a brick store structure of Augusta County, now an apartment building.

67

*(Opposite page) Two empty store structures, each housing several shops, quietly await their fate (top) in Buena Vista and (bottom) in Botetourt County. This large building (right) remains open as a general store in the town of Monterey. One of the tallest stores I've encountered, it also has a built-in elevator. The compact building, (below) though once a country store, now provides the community of Goshen with space for the town office and a branch library.*

*Pictured here is a small country store building in Greene County (above), a former store building housing a fraternal organization in Augusta County (right), and a country store in Albemarle County (below), as it appeared in the late 1960s.*

*[Tr]ue to the rectangular shape, these [small]-town store buildings offer very [di]fferent facades. The store (right) [in] Saluda is strikingly deceptive, for [it] now serves the public as an antique mini-mall. The stores below [re]main open, but not as general [st]ores, (bottom left) in Shenandoah [an]d (right) in Grottoes.*

*In the 1920s, many merchants responded to the new opportunities for profit offered by the automobile. Gasoline pumps began appearing at stores in even the most remote rural areas of the state. Store (below) on a dirt road of Greene County is as it appeared in the 1960s.*

# WHEN MERCHANTS PUMPED THE GAS

*(Above) This merchant in Isle of Wight County cleverly built a small canopy over his gas pumps, rather than a large extension, as did the store owner (below) of Sussex County. Was this Texaco merchant the forerunner of our present era of covered pumps?*

*Automobiles and the gasoline pump have greatly altered the look of many country stores. On the following pages are a variety of country stores showing methods used in housing their pumps. (Above) Still open and selling gas is this store in King William County. (Below) An old store, this is open only as a Post Office in Madison County.*

*This merchant in Upperville (above) built an addition and attached his canopy to the addition. The general store (below) at Bells Crossroads in Louisa County still enjoys a good run of trade.*

Pictured are two store buildings which appear to be abandoned gasoline stations, but their size indicates otherwise. The rare brick store building (above) is in Nottoway County and (below) the store structure is in King and Queen County.

*This delightful little country store (above) is in Highland County. Note the unique "Y" support in front. Gasoline pump reads "34 cents per gallon". Wooden store (below) in King and Queen County now serves as a storage barn.*

*Three old stores with covered pump areas minus the pumps: (Opposite top) a Churchville store in Augusta County, (opposite bottom) a book store in the quaint old community of Brownsburg, Rockbridge County, and (above) a deserted store in Port Royal. A country store (below) in Madison County pictured as it appeared in the 1970s.*

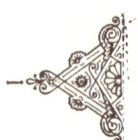 *When tea rooms were still in fashion, a few merchants offered refreshments while refilling the autos with gasoline. The store building (above) in King William County even concealed gas pumps inside brick pillars supporting the canopy. (Below) A store and tea room, now demolished, stood in Albemarle County.*

# A POTPOURRI OF STORES

*The following stores were a bit difficult to classify in terms used previously for a variety of reasons. Some are empty, others are open with an interesting mix of merchants, and several remain as genuine country stores. (Right) An empty shell sits in Nelson County, (below) a former store with attached Post Office is now an antique shop in Orange County.*

*This store building (above) in Halifax County was deceiving. The sign said antiques, but the interior clearly showed its origin as a country store. The graceful lines of the structure (below) in Surry County are frequently found on similar stores in the surrounding countryside.*

 *Wyant's General Store (above) in Albemarle County has remained in business for over a hundred years. This Sussex County store (below) sits by the roadside mournfully awaiting its fate.*

*(Far left) Store building of the past struggles to merchandise old items of the past. (Left) An empty store waits by a railroad track in Sussex County. (Left below) The original store burned and this structure was built in the 1920s as a copy of the first. This sits in Nelson County near the James River. (Right) An old store is now serving as a restaurant in Rappahannock County. In the foothills of the Blue Ridge, the country store (below) served a community, which was once a railroad town.*

*This is a once-proud general store (above) of Madison County. (Below) A country store still serves customers in western Loudoun County.*

*Currently open (above) and still going strong is a neat little store in Nelson County with a view of the mountains. (Below) A quaint store building of Highland County now is open only as a Post Office.*

Here are two stores in decline, (left) in Rockbridge County and (below) in the mountains of Madison County. (Opposite right) At one time a country store/Post Office, this Sussex County building serves area customers in a different capacity. (Opposite below) The country store pictured here, open to people in the Fairy Stone Park area, retains old glass showcases from the past.

The diminutive country store (left) was found in Nelson County. The store building (below) was once the pride of a community in Albemarle County. The intriguing store (opposite right) in Carroll County is now an antique shop. The gasoline pumps and signs, though not original with the store, add color. (Opposite below) Sitting near the confluence of two rivers, this 20th Century country store of Rockingham County offers an unusual variety of challenges for sportsmen.

*The store (above) in Southampton County has my vote for the most unusual. (Right) This is a vacant store of Orange County. A store, (below) also of Orange County, is typical of many country stores that were also 4th Class Post Offices. When their owners turned 70, the U. S. Postal Service retired them as postmasters, closed the Post Offices therein and effectively shut down the stores. Without government support, they could not remain profitable. (Opposite) These two stores closed years ago, (top) in Madison County and (below) in Augusta County.*

*I am always saddened by the sight of old store buildings that have been abandoned and left to the elements. Yet, I felt it necessary to record what did remain of some once proud enterprises. I had the privilege of visiting a few of them before their decline.*

## IN SILENT SURRENDER

4

5

*Here are some examples from around the state: (1) Sussex County, (2) Louisa County, (3) Hanover County, (4) Caroline County, (5) Botetourt County, (6) Buckingham County.*

6

Soon after the flood of 1969 in Central Virginia, I took this picture of what appeared to be a late 18th Century store building removed from its foundation near the James River. Returning 25 years later, in hopes of finding the old building restored to its original location, I was disappointed to find only these fragmented remains (below and right).

*This derelict country store (above) sits in Southampton County. The shell of this general store (below) wastes away in Fluvanna County close to the James River.*

*The four old store buildings pictured here all bear a resemblance to stores of the late 18th and early 19th Century: (1) a well-preserved store in Augusta County, (2) a large building adjacent to the mountains in Albemarle County, (3) demolished soon after the photo was taken, this building stood in Orange County, (4) and this store was found in Fluvanna County.*

R. DUFF GREEN

99

*(Right) Once enjoying a very prosperous run of trade, this large general store structure sits quietly beside a busy highway in Western Rockingham County. (Below and below right) Here are the disintegrating remains of a company store built by a vanished railroad in Southampton County. (Bottom) Deep in the mountains of Nelson County, this old store slowly yields to the elements.*

# GOING...
## GOING...

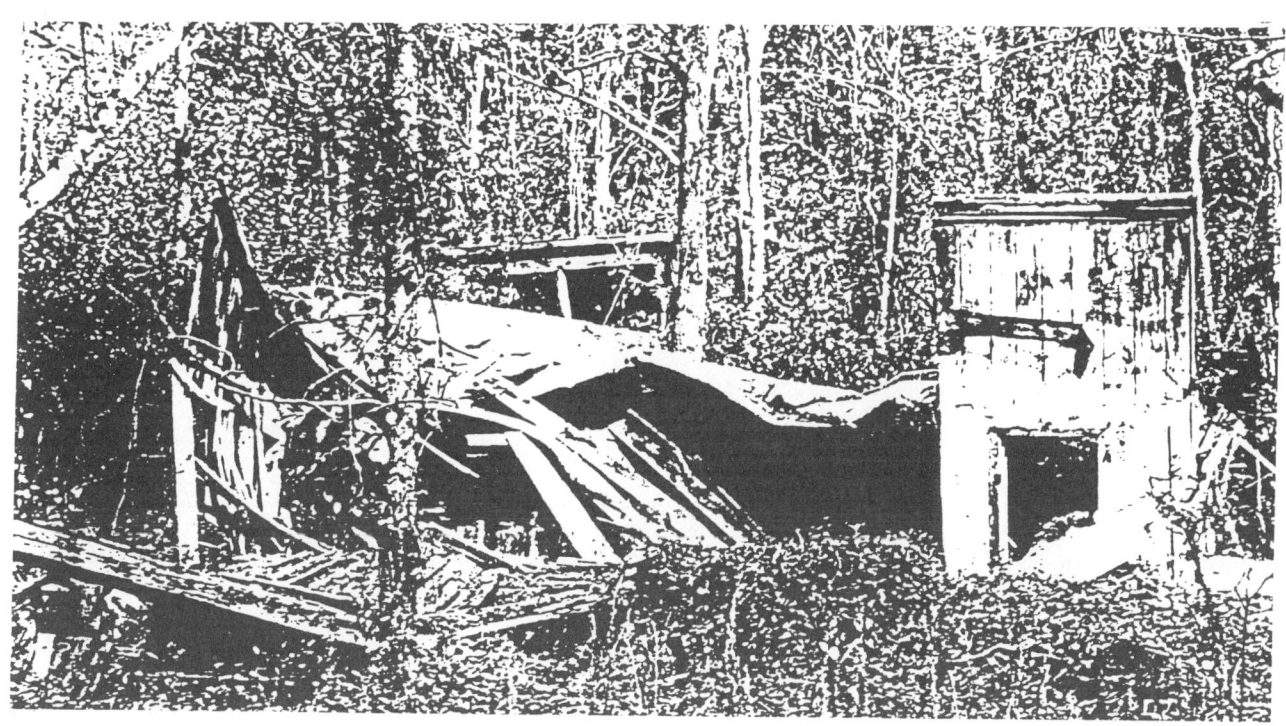

*Morse's Gen'l Store first appeared in a downstairs room of our home in Orange County. Pictured in the early 1970s is the "storekeeper" and his then-young family.*

WILLIAM ALBERT ALLARD

# CHAPTER 4  RECREATING AN OLD COUNTRY STORE

My collection of country store items began in the 1960s as an afterthought. A graphic designer by profession, my work required making frequent trips to the nation's capital. On the return trips home, I followed a variety of Virginia routes, backroads, and byways looking for country stores. To help remember a store's location, I began purchasing old and outdated items from the merchant's dwindling stock. With these items as memory building blocks, I began collecting on film old store buildings, which would eventually include more than 150 stores from around the Old Dominion.

In one old country store, I found a wealth of inventory still on the shelves. This store, on the back street of a small town, had enjoyed a good run of trade through four or five decades. But it had experienced the ultimate decline suffered by almost all country stores unable to compete with super markets and specialty stores prices.

For over a year, I purchased out-of-date merchandise from this store. One of my most valued acquisitions was a group of store inventories, spanning many years between the two World Wars. This became my guide for seeking old merchandise. Frequently, I returned to stores previously visited looking for additional items noted from the old inventories. After a while, the room which I was using for storage became quite crowded. Then, when I acquired several old show cases, the collection began haphazardly filling one of our outbuildings.

Sensing the obvious, which somehow had escaped me, my wife said, "Why not take our library room and turn it into a country store!"

This to me was a moment of profound joy. How often is a husband really certain of how a wife views his hobbies and interests? In a rela-

tively short time, "Morse's Gen'l Store" became a reality in the first of its many locations.

In the early 1970s I was working for an area newspaper part-time, which allowed me the freedom to search out more old country stores. The collection outgrew our library and filled an outbuilding again.

In a rare coincidence, I got word that a very large old country store I'd visited several years before was being converted to an antique mall. After a short period of negotiations, Morse's Gen'l Store next appeared as an attraction in the old country store antique mall.

At this time, another old store building

BACKROADS MAGAZINE

*This is a portion of the patent medicine collection containing about 150 different potions and cure-alls. The shelves were several thicknesses of cardboard which produced the appropriate sag so often seen in older country stores.*

near our home was being converted to apartments and I obtained a number of store counters dating to the 1880s. The countertops were in poor condition, but again I lucked out. In a nearby town, a much older building was enjoying restoration. Being discarded were inner wall partitions of rough cut planks of heart poplar 14 to 16 inches wide. After persistent persuasion, the owner of a neighborhood lumber company finally agreed to plane down one side of these rough old planks. They made beautiful counter top replacements.

With the advent of the national celebration of our Bicentennial, I became part of a small group formed to establish a museum to honor James Madison, a Founding Father who had made his home in our county.

Madison, along with Thomas Jefferson, had been a strong proponent of the science of agriculture, a labor of the mind as well as the body. The museum, through a very fortunate legacy,

 *The two pictures (below and opposite) were taken at the front of our country store as displayed at the James Madison Museum in the Town of Orange during the Bicentennial Celebration in 1976.*

was able to purchase a building suitable for our purpose. As far as historical material and items, we had almost nothing. But since our basic theme was agriculture, we decided to stretch that to include for display an old country store, which I just happened to have available. So for the Bicentennial Celebration period, Morse's Gen'l Store enjoyed a "brisk run of trade" in the form of visitors as part of the museum.

Next, a career move for my wife, a chamber of commerce executive, took us to the Shenandoah Valley. Morse's Gen'l Store followed us and experienced several more locations. Once again, I built shelves, moved counters, and condensed the store into a downstairs room of our home.

After packing and repacking, taking apart and reassembling various items, cataloguing and re-cataloguing, planning and rebuilding stands and displays, I said, "Enough is enough! This store must find a permanent home."

Fortunately, about the time I was making the decision about my country store collection, the State Fair of Virginia was expanding its permanent exhibition, "Heritage Village", to include a series of early shops and an old country store. That the Fair and I got together is history.

In its opening year at the State Fair of Virginia, the country store enjoyed thousands of visitors, very rewarding news for this collector of old country stores and the everyday items that graced their shelves.

# HERITAGE VILLAGE COUNTRY STORE

History unfolds each year for thousands of Virginia elementary school students as they are guided through this country store and the other authentic shops, exhibits, and demonstrations that are an integral part of Heritage Village at State Fair time in August and September.

Inside the store, shelves and counters are brimming with merchandise of the past, along with display cases and a vast array of other store memorabilia that provide the atmosphere of an era gone by.

Located on the grounds of the Virginia State Fair Complex at Richmond's Strawberry Hill, the old country store enjoys between 75,000 and 100,000 visitors annually during State Fair Days.

*Many a farmer passed his long winter leisure hours over a checker board beside an old pot-bellied stove. This tradition is carried on here at the country store (below) as visitors are encouraged to "set a spell" and enjoy a game or two of checkers.*

# COUNTRY STORE SCRAP BOOK

*In searching out country stores through the years, I've managed to collect an interesting assortment of paper relating to stores and the business of doing business. Included here are random examples from a variety of sources pertaining to stores in general, not just Virginia stores.*

*I found it difficult to interperse and relate these items to my earlier narrative without getting overly detailed or wordy, so I decided to group them in this section. With short introductory comments, I felt they could tell their own story.*

## ADVERTISING

*Country merchants were far more conservative with money spent for advertising than in-town storekeepers for one good reason. They had a captive audience. Most in-town merchants had competition, and advertising helped define their differences.*

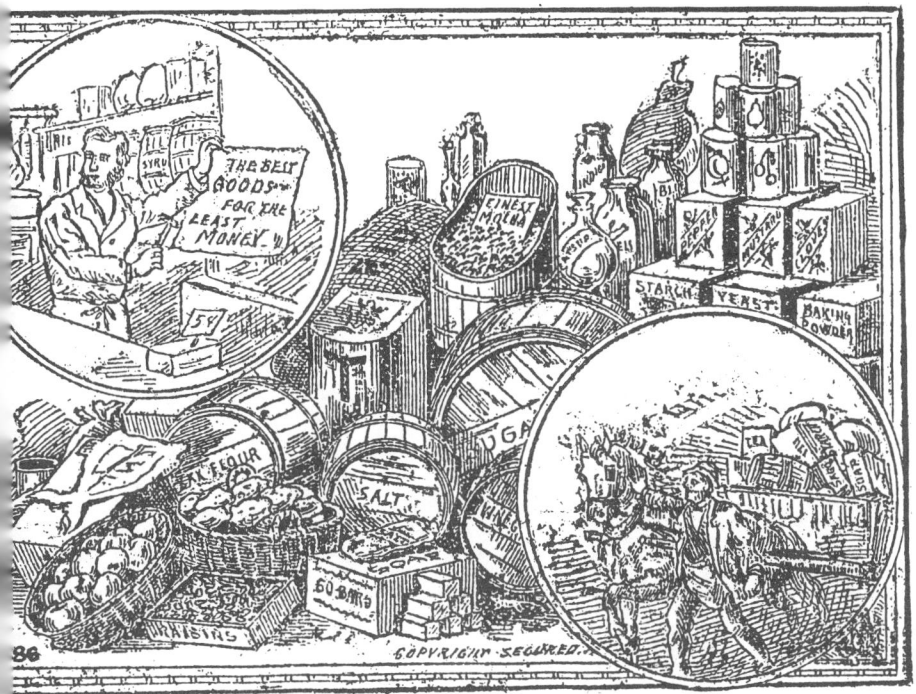

JOHN H. TATE,
Grocer and Confectioner,

**WANTED**

Why wait two or three weeks
for the returns of

**FURS?**

BRING THEM TO

**C. HAGERTY**

HIGHEST CASH PRICE PAID FOR SAME

ORANGE  :-:  VIRGINIA

## ADVERTISING cont.

*After the Civil War, many prepackaged products came on the market and manufacturers discovered that an excellent way to reach customers was to advertise in the newspapers. This also got the attention of the merchants. (Opposite page) Here are some ads typical of those placed by in-town shopkeepers during the 1800s.*

### "A Perfect Sight!"

Those "horrid pimples" are sure to disappear if you will purify your blood by the use of

### Ayer's Sarsaparilla.

"We regard Ayer's Sarsaparilla as a real blessing. For pimples and eruptions of almost every description, it is a positive cure. We have kept it in our family for the past twenty years." — Mrs. J. W. COCKRELL, Alexandria, Va.

### Ayer's Sarsaparilla

**Rex Brand Cudahy's Extract of Beef**

Send 6c in stamps for postage on sample package, mailed free. Manufactured by

**THE CUDAHY PACKING CO., SOUTH OMAHA, NEB.**

---

**OLD STAG WHISKEY**
HALL & HUME
SOLE PROP'S
WASHINGTON, DIST. OF COL.

IN GLASS OR WOOD.
PER GAL. $6.00
PER CASE $18.00
A LIBERAL DISCOUNT TO THE TRADE.

This Whiskey has a national reputation and is unrivalled for Smoothness, Flavor and Purity, and for the Sideboard or sickroom is unequalled.

*Packed and shipped to any part of the Country, free of charge.*

**BANKER'S IMPROVED KEG.**
PATENTED OCT. 11TH 1859.

**BANKER & CARPENTER, SOLE PROPRIETORS. BOSTON.**

WE are prepared to offer every description of WHITE LEAD and ZINC WHITE, (ground in oil,) without any extra charge, in "Banker's Patent Kegs," of 25, 50, and 100 pounds each; and Colors of all kinds in kegs of 20, 40, and 80 lbs each. These Kegs have an *extra coating of Shellac Varnish on the inside*, which effectually prevents leakage, or the wood absorbing the oil. They can be readily converted into paint Buckets or pails, each keg being furnished with ears, and a suitable bail, which is sprung into the bottom, and is not liable to injury by rough handling while in transit. These kegs can be unheaded by removing ONLY the upper hoop, (as the head rests on a shoulder instead of entering a groove,) and inserting an end of the bail in the staple on the head.

All orders addressed as above will receive prompt attention. eplm sept 7

---

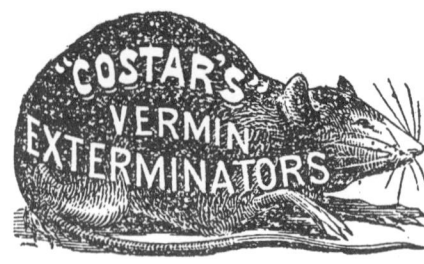

**COSTAR'S VERMIN EXTERMINATORS**

THE ONLY INFALLIBLE REMEDIES KNOWN.

Destroys Instantly

EVERY FORM AND SPECIES OF

## VERMIN.

**ST. JACOBS OIL**
TRADE MARK

THE GREAT
**GERMAN REMEDY FOR PAIN.**

CURES
Rheumatism, Neuralgia, Sciatica, Lumbago, Backache, Headache, Toothache, Sore Throat, Swellings, Sprains, Bruises, Burns, Scalds, Frost Bites, AND ALL OTHER BODILY PAINS AND ACHES.
Sold by Druggists and Dealers everywhere. Fifty Cents a bottle. Directions in 11 languages.
THE CHARLES A. VOGELER CO.
(Successors to A. VOGELER & CO.) Baltimore, Md., U. S. A.

ONE BOTTLE of Perry Davis's Pain Killer
Will often do Wonders for a Whole Family!
TRY IT!
25c., 50c, or $1.

---

**RAVEN SHOE**
Absolutely the best. Softens and preserves leather. Makes ladies' shoes look *new*, not varnished.
**BUTTON & OTTLEY,**

**Button's RAVEN GLOSS SHOE DRESSING**

**GLOSS DRESSING**
Leading Shoe Dealers everywhere commend it. Is economical. Take no other. Beware of imitations.
Mfrs., NEW YORK.

## New Spring Goods.

### ARCHIBALD HART,

HAS just received a handsome assortment of FRESH GOODS, which he will sell unusually low for Cash:

AMONGST THEM ARE,

**Irish Linens, Long Lawns,**
Cheap colored and white Domestics,
Blue and Yellow Nankeens,
Marseilles Vestings,
Cloths, Cassimeres, Cambrics, Muslins,
Brown Linens, Calicoes and Ginghams,
Canton Crapes, Crape Shawls, &c. &c.

ALSO,
Loaf and Brown Sugar, Tea, Coffee, Pepper, Alspice, Ginger, Nutmegs, and almost every other article in the

*Dry Goods, Hardware and Grocery Line.*

April 19.     6t

---

### ☞ REMOVAL.

### W. Redd & Co.

RESPECTFULLY inform their friends and acquaintances, that they have removed to Commerce Street, (in the house lately in the occupancy of Mr. Wm. S. Stone,) where they offer for sale,

*An extensive Assortment of*

**Dry Goods, Hardware,**

AND

## GROCERIES;

All of which they are determined to sell on good terms.

They avail themselves of this opportunity to express their gratitude for past favours, and shall be thankful for a continuance of the same.

☞ Cash given for good Wheat.

Fred'g, March 22, 1820.     tf

---

### The Subscribers,

WOULD inform their friends and the public generally, that they have formed a connexion in business under the firm of

### GOW & CRISMOND,

And have taken the Store recently occupied by Messrs. Wm. Redd & Co. where they intend keeping a general assortment of

### GROCERIES,

Which will be sold very low for Cash; and hope by assiduity and attention to business, to merit a share of public patronage.

Jno. L. Gow,
H. B. Crismond.

April 19, 1820.     tf

---

## SODA,

AND

*Other Mineral Waters ;*

And will keep a regular supply through the season at the above named Establishment, adjoining the Chancery Office.

*James Cooke.*

---

### COFFMANS & BRUFFY.

1866!     **A NEW YEAR**     1866!

HAS OPENED UPON US

with its

HOPES, RESPONSIBILITIES AND TRIALS,

AND

EVERYBODY WILL BE ANXIOUS TO KNOW

where to get

THE GREATEST AMOUNT OF GOODS

FOR

**THE SMALLEST SUM OF MONEY.**

WE HAVE ON HAND

## ANY AMOUNT OF NEW GOODS,

and

WE MEAN TO SELL THEM

IN

☞ HARRISONBURG. ☜

THEY WERE BOUGHT UPON GOOD TERMS

and will most certainly be sold,

UPON EQUALLY SATISFACTORY TERMS.

LET THE PEOPLE CALL AND SEE

whether the

Cheapest Goods in Town

Are not to be found

AT

OUR     HOUSE.

WE WILL NOT ENUMERATE.

WE WANT THE PEOPLE TO TRY US!

IF OUR MERCHANDISE IS NOT

**GOOD AND CHEAP,**

DON'T BUY IT;

IF IT IS TRY IT!

The public's already greatly obliged and humble servants,

COFFMANS & BRUFFY.

---

### SADDLERY,

of all kinds, and cheap.

**Hardware,**

Queensware, &c.,

in great variety,

AND AT CHEAPEST RATES.

### Boots and Shoes,

A NEW STOCK

JUST RECEIVED AND FOR SALE BY

**COFFMANS & BRUFFY.**

Harrisonburg, Feb. 17. 1866.

---

We are now

## OPENING

AT THE OLD STAND.

—AT—

### MILNES, VA,

The largest and Best Stock of

*General Merchandise,*

That has been brought to this place for years past.

It consists, in part of

## DRY GOODS,

In Great Variety.

**READY-MADE CLOTHING,**

For Men and Boys.

A large Stock of

**Boots and Shoes.**

Hats and Caps,

Notions,

## GROCERIES,

Best Quality.

*PROVISIONS,*

Drugs and Medicines,

Tobacco, Cigars,

Confections;

—also—

## HARDWARE,

Glass and Queensware

Stationery, etc.

All of which, we will sell at

LOW PRICES.

If we haven't what you want in Stock, we will order it.

Come and see us.

**B. & T. J. MILNES.**

# THE WAY TO BUY
# GOODS CHEAP!

In consequence of the recent excitement in this vicinity among those having to purchase Goods, in regard to the advantages claimed by the

## "UNION STORES"

Over others doing a Credit Business, that, no credit being given, Goods can be sold at a

## MUCH LESS PER CENT. PROFIT!

In view of this fact, and believing that this principle will meet with the cordial approbation of all who ever intend to pay for what they buy, I have determined to

## RELINQUISH THE CREDIT SYSTEM,

And commence with a fresh assortment of GOODS, and sell them for

## READY PAY ONLY,

AND WILL ENDEAVOR TO BUY

## DRY GOODS!
## GROCERIES,
## CROCKERY AND HARDWARE,

At such prices that I can sell them as Cheap as the Cheapest.

## J. A. SWEETMAN.

Charlton, 1852.

OLIVER & BROTHER, Steam Printers, 20 Nassau-Street, N.Y.

---

# FREE FREE

HIGH GRADE
Natural Tone
TALKING and
SINGING
MACHINE
**FREE**

Call at our Store and hear the specially prepared Records of Bands and other instrumental Music, Songs, Stories, Recitations, etc., and assure yourself that this is the best offered. You Buy Only the Records

THESE RECORDS ARE FAMOUS FOR THEIR TONE AND QUALITY

As a home entertainer it has no equal. The best talent in the country is brought right to your fireside to while away the long evenings with comical recitations and songs. An impromptu dance may be gotten up at a moment's notice and here you have the best orchestra of the country to play the dance music. Or you may wish to learn a song–no what better instructor can you have than one of the Peerless singers to phrase a song over and over again if need be. The possibilities of this wonderful little machine for instruction and amusement are endless.

### DESCRIPTION OF INSTRUMENT

THE CABINET—Made of heavy, solid oak throughout. Corner posts are made with fluted mouldings.
SHIELED TONE ARM—The latest triumph of scientific research, producing the largest volume and purest tone quality, eliminating the metallic scratch so common in the ordinary type of machine.
THE MOTOR—Of special strength and construction, unusually durable.
TURN TABLE—Ten inch diameter, accomodating any size disc record.
STANDARD ANALYZING REPRODUCER Sound flush-Insuring the most perfect reproduction of any known sound; fitted with automatic needle clamp, permitting of the instant releasing or fastening of the needle.
SPEED REGULATOR—Permitting the ready adjustment of the speed to suit the individual fancy or requirements, such as for dance music or speaking records.
FLOWER HORN—Seventeen inches in length, with a fifteen inch flared bell. Finished in a beautiful, deep, rich red enamel, and decorated with gold stripes.

One Standard Talking Machine with Handsome Flower Horn $25.00
FREE to every Customer whose Cash Purchases amount to

See and hear this wonderful instrument and learn how easily you can obtain one
One Machine to a Home

## BATES & VROMAN
GENERAL MERCHANDISE
Groceries, Dry Goods, Notions, Boots and Shoes, Woodenware and Tinware

---

## ADVERTISING cont.

Handbills (both above) were a popular form of advertising for merchants all through the 1800s. An early 1900s printed piece (left) was on brown store wrapping paper. (Page opposite) Newspaper advertisements and flyers were sent to merchants offering special incentives.

---

# G. BEAR,
*Millinery,*

DRY GOODS, NOTIONS, SHOES, HAT

Clothing, Trunks and Groceries.

## GORDONSVILLE, VA

# Bad Roads HELD UP Our BIG Sale

Folks are just now able to get here, and let me tell you they are coming!

Therefore Sale will continue **to March 15** 1926 with same low prices as advertised in this paper.

## J. L. Whitlock
### WOLFTOWN, VA.

## Use Our Values to Put On a Sale of Your Own
### We Do More Than Just "Meet" Prices—WE BEAT PRICES
### Use Our A. W. C. Advertising System Circulars to Advertise Your Values

|  |  |
|---|---|
| Japanese 12-momme Pongee, red stamp. Yd. | $.33½ |
| Womens Full Fashioned Pure Thread Silk Hose . Doz. | 9.25 |
| Ripplette Bedspreads (63x90 Each, 72x90 Each, 81x90 Each) | 8¾ / 1¼ / 1.25 |
| Gillette Safety Razor Blades 5 in pkg. Pkg. | .28 |
| Gillette Safety Razor Blades 10 in pkg. Pkg. | .56 |
| Lord Baltimore Guaranteed Nickel Alarm Clocks. Ea. | .60 |
| Druid 9/4 Brown Sheeting . . . Yd. | .33½ |
| Truth 36-in. Bleached Muslin 10-pc. cart.Yd. | .11⅜ |
| Truth 36-in. Bleached Muslin Less than cart.Yd. | .11½ |
| D2502, 32-in. Rayon and Cotton Mixture Suiting . Yd. | .10½ |
| Manchester Chambrays, Stripes or Solids 10/20-yd. lengths. Yd. | .07⅝ |
| E9029 22x44 4/5 lb. Turkish Towels, Colored Borders . Dz. | 2.05 |
| L700, Mens White Hdkfs. Each in Envelope. Doz. | .43 |
| GS34, Mens 2.20 Denim Overalls or Coats.Dz. | 9.95 |
| L3608, Womens Pressed Crepe Bloomers,Dz. | 2.10 |
| Mennen's Talcum Powder . . . Doz. | 1.46 |
| 2-qt. Gray Enameled Coffee Pot . Doz. | 2.25 |
| 13½-in. Gray Enameled Wash Bowl. Doz. | $1.75 |
| 4-qt. Aluminum Sa... | |
| 4-string Floor Broo... | |
| Homer Laughlin Sem... | |
| 10-qt. White Enam... | |
| 808 Bicycle Playin... | |
| Beechnut Chewing... | |
| B4985 & B4986, M... | |
| Rubber Sole Trim... | |
| B3587, Mens Stur... | |
| Defiance 46-in. O... | |
| Ideal Hit & Miss ... | |
| A.W.C. Felt Base... | |
| Blue Banner Tube... | |
| M5896, Mens .50c... | |

### American Wholesale Corpo...
### BALTIMORE, MARYLAND

## BIG TEN DAY SALE

WE MUST HAVE LOWER PRICES. Our Dealers have given us a Small Cut on some things we have in Stock.

AMONG THESE THINGS ARE THE "STAR BRAND SHOES", A GUARANTEED ALL LEATHER SHOE, ONE OF THE BEST SHOES ON THE MARKET.

Come and see for yourself we have our goods marked as low as any merchant and very much lower than some we are going to prove- we are willing to divide our discount with you, on every pair of Shoes or boots we sell from the 10th to the 19th we will give back 50c cash or goods on every pair of our shoes and arctics will give back 15c cash or goods.

WE also have a full line of Boys Suits which we will give $1.00 cash or goods on every suit sold.

We wish to call your attention to extreme low prices on Groceries.

|  |  |
|---|---|
| Tomatoes per can | 16c |
| Peaches per can | 25c |
| Pineapple per can | 30c |
| Apple butter per can | 23c |
| Preserves large can | 24c |
| Salmon two can | 24c |
| Herring two can | 23c |
| Fish Roe large can | 23c |
| Pork and Beans per can from | 9 to 14c |
| The very best western meat per pound | 15c |
| Sugar per pound | 6c |

### H. A. TAYLOR & COMPANY,    Barboursville, Va.

The two periodical ads (left and above) could be described as "trickle up" advertising. The customer is motivated to request the items from his merchant. If he does not carry the item, the merchant is motivated to acquire it from this supplier and so on. (Above) Examples of price tags from the 1930s and 1940s.

# PAPERS & PAPERWORK

*The success of any merchant greatly depended on his attention to detail, especially in bookkeeping. The records of general merchants often reveal the triumphs and tragedies of every day life through the simple medium of arithmetic. This blacksmithing account was included in the records of a general merchant.*

Albany, February 1, 1874

Commenced business with the following
resources and liabilities, taken from
the Balance Sheet of Ledger K.

── Resources. ──

| | | | |
|---|---|---|---|
| Cash on hand, | $1822.20 | | |
| Notes " | 171.50 | | |
| Robert Barker's account, | 550.00 | | |
| Henry Ivison's " | 222.50 | | |
| J. C. Bryant's " | 186.00 | | |
| S. Fairbanks " | 293.75 | 3045 | 95 |

── Liabilities ──

| | | | |
|---|---|---|---|
| Our Note, favor of James Dunn, | $2500.00 | 2500 | |

Bot. of Springer and Whitman, on ⅔.
| | | | | |
|---|---|---|---|---|
| 20 Bags Rio Coffee, 1670 lbs., | @15¢ | $250.50 | | |
| 15 Tierces Rice, 7500 " | " 4¢ | 300.00 | | |
| 15 Hhds. Cuba Sugar, 14000 lbs., | " 5¢ | 700.00 | 1250 | 50 |

Bot. of Alex Cowley, for Cash,
| | | | | |
|---|---|---|---|---|
| 12 Hhds. N.O. Molasses, 720 gal. | @40¢ | $288.00 | | |
| 20 Boxes Soap, 1450 lbs., | " 8¢ | 116.00 | | |
| 10 Bbls. Pork, 2000 " | " 10¢ | 200.00 | 604 | |

Sold James Lyman, on ⅔,
| | | | | |
|---|---|---|---|---|
| 50 lbs. Coffee, | @18¢ | $5.40 | | |
| 20 " Rice, | " 5½¢ | 1.10 | | |
| 100 " Sugar, | " 6¢ | 6.00 | 12 | 50 |

Rec'd Cash on Personal a/c, equally ⅔, | | | 350 | |

Paid Cash on Sundry unincidentally expenses, | | | 90 | |

| | | 7782 | 95 |

---

Blacksmith account.

Mr. R. D. Browning

| | | |
|---|---|---|
| Mch. 20-19 | Cost of tire | .70 |
| " " " | " " spokes | .50 |
| " " " | work on spokes | 1.25 |
| " " " | " " tire | 1.00 |
| Apr. 6 | Cost of material for wagon | 5.00 |
| " " | work on tires, setting | 2.00 |
| " " | " " Rims | 3.00 |
| " " | Shoeing | 1.25 |
| " " | " | .33 |
| " " | " | .63 |
| May 2 | " | |
| May 21 | cost of tire for buggy | 2.10 |
| " " | tire work | 3.00 |
| | 4 spokes | 1.00 |
| | cutting 1 tire | .60 |
| | ½ Rims work | .50 |
| June 14 | Shoeing | .33 |
| July 28 | Cost of Rim | .50 |
| | " " tires | .84 |
| | work on Rim | 1.00 |
| | " " tire | 1.00 |
| | Two spokes | .50 |
| Aug 14 | To 1 shoe | .33 |
| " 16 | 5 spokes | 2.25 |
| " 16 | cutting 3 tires | 1.80 |
| Sept 5 | To work on buggy | .78 |
| | Total amt $32.19 | |

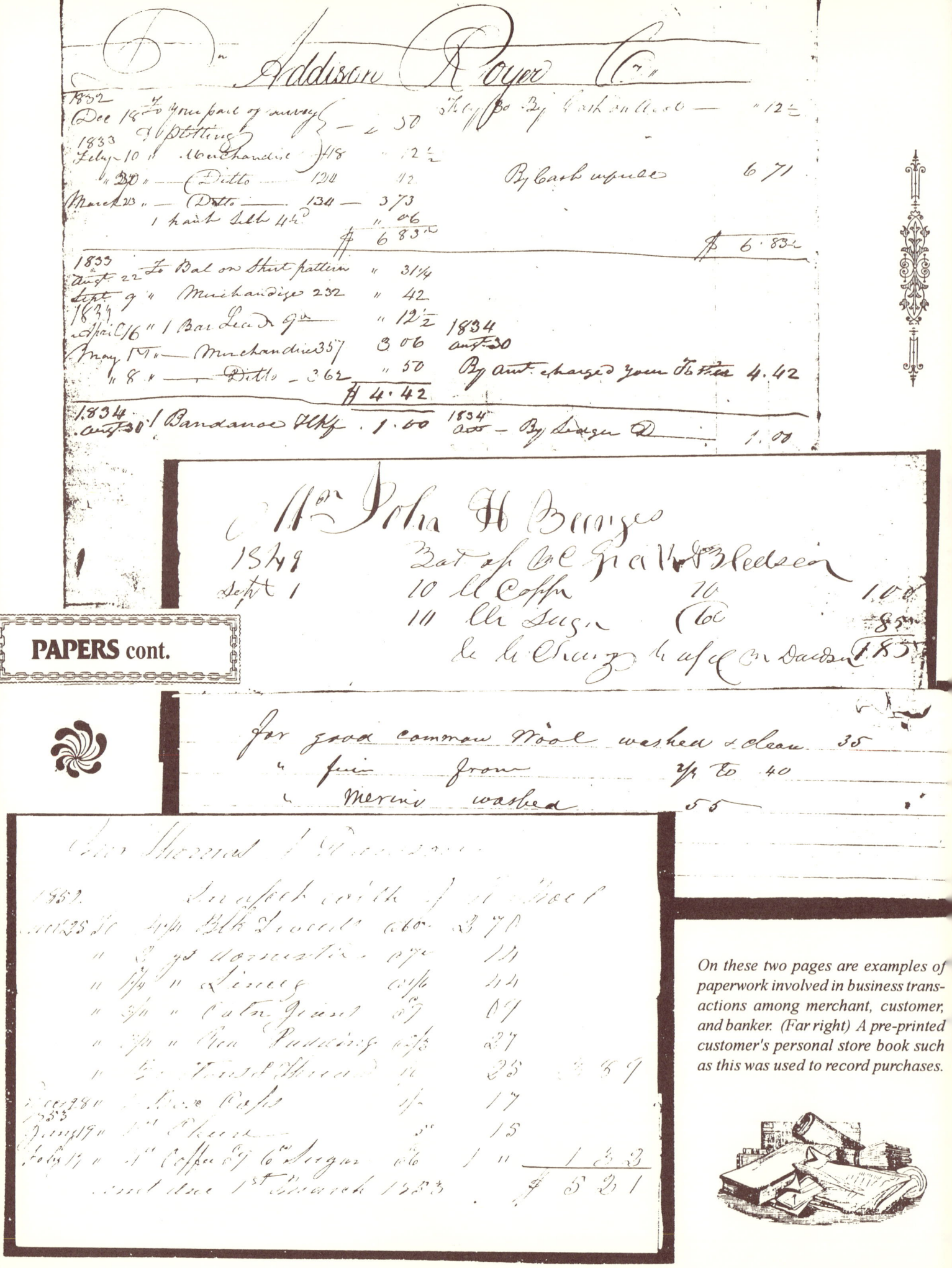

*On these two pages are examples of paperwork involved in business transactions among merchant, customer, and banker. (Far right) A pre-printed customer's personal store book such as this was used to record purchases.*

**C. V. Beckman,**
*Dealer in*
*General Merchandise.*

Bayard, W. Va., Oct 7th 1903

Amt Due the following People for Labor to Date
John Gay 26½ days @ 1.75 to Date   46 37
Sam Gay 25 days @ 1.50 to Date   37 50
Geo Gay 23 days @ 1.50 to Date   34 50
                                    $118 37

Mr G P Shaffer Please Pay the above Parties
Each the amt opsite their Names And Charg Same to
me on Sawing

Chas Locke

---

STATEMENT.    Prompt Payments Make Good Credit

Woodstock, Va., 3/31 1916

Mr J. C. Adkerson
        Woodstock Va.

**To T. GLENN LOCKE, Dr.**
*Dealer in*
DRY GOODS, NOTIONS, GROCERIES, BOOTS,
SHOES, HATS, CAPS, &c., &c.

1916
Mch 2  To Iron                    35
  23   Oranges 30 Candy 10        40
       Eggs 72 Sugar 40          1 12
                                 $3 04

Received Payment March 4, 1916
        T. Glenn Locke
            Per G S A

RECEIVED BY _____
PRICE APPROVED BY _____
TO BE USED BY _____

---

ALWAYS BRING THIS BOOK.

M _____

*In account with*

**DEALER IN**

**FINE GROCERIES,**

FLOUR of all Grades.
Selected Teas, Pure Coffees and Spices.
Butter and Cheese from Best Dairies.
CHOICE SYRUP AND MOLASSES.
FOREIGN AND DOMESTIC FRUITS.
Canned Fruits in Variety.
Also a complete Assortment of Goods usually
kept in a First Class Store.

Goods Delivered Promptly, Free of Expense.

*The sketches were made of counters I found in a variety of stores. The slant-in front on counters was for the benefit of women in long, flowing dresses prior to the 1900s. The store stoves represent the extreme styles to be found from the large and very ornate to the simple converted steel barrel.*

# STORE FIXTURES

*After the Civil War, aspiring store owners could choose from a variety of offerings from companies aiding them in setting up or modernizing their stores. These illustrations (below) are from the catalogues of the 1900s. Most country merchants would simply nail shelving to the wall and avoid the expense of moveable shelving.*

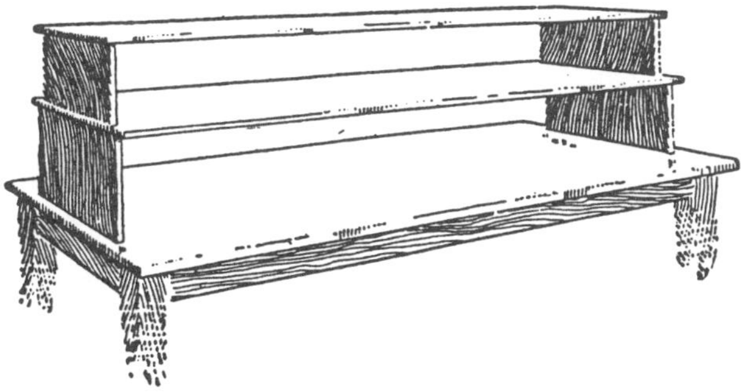

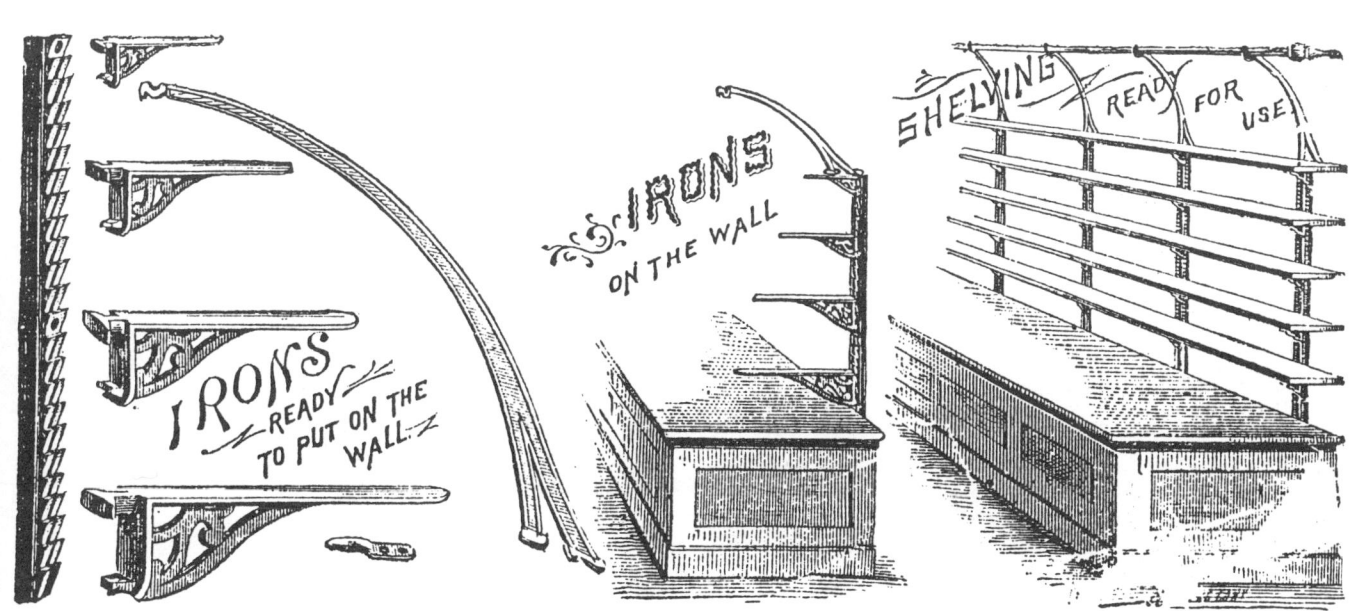

J. W. Patton's Patent Adjustable Ratchet Bar and Bracket Store Shelving Irons.

## WHOLESALE HOUSES

In the aftermath of war, there usually follows a period of great manufacturing using the technology spawned by the conflict. This was quite true after the Civil War. Manufacturers and wholesalers multiplied and spread across the land. Drummers with their catalogues became the merchants' best ally.

**Gilbert Bros. & Co.**
Wholesale Druggists
9 North Ho[ward]

JNO. JAY GILBERT.
WILLIAM B. GILBERT.

Shipped to Agt. Somerset
Sold to
Via. S. R. R

| | | |
|---|---|---|
| 1 | Dozen | No. 7 S. M. Oil |
| 10 | Pound | Alum |
| 10 | " | Sulphur |
| ½ | Dozen | Pierce's res... |

Baltimore, June 8 1881

Messrs J N Aylor & Bro

BOUGHT OF **J. HENRY REIP & CO.,**
MANUFACTURERS & JOBBERS OF
**TIN WARE, AND DEALERS IN STOVES,**
JAPANNED, STAMPED and HOLLOW WARE.

FACTORY, 26 MARION ST. NEW NUMBER 220 FAYETTE ST., NEAR HOWARD.

EXCELSIOR—Hot Blast.

| | | | | |
|---|---|---|---|---|
| ½ Dz | 2 qt | Cov'd Buckets | 75 | 38 |
| ½ Dz | 4 qt | " | 1.50 | 75 |
| ⅓ Dz | 1 qt | Coffee Pots | 1.00 | 33 |
| ⅓ Dz | 2 qt | " " | 1.40 | 47 |
| ⅓ Dz | 3 qt | " " | 1.65 | 55 |

## AMERICAN WHOLESALE CORPORATION
(BALTIMORE BARGAIN HOUSE)
ESTABLISHED 1881
PAID IN CAPITAL - THIRTEEN MILLION DOLLARS

MANUFACTURERS OF
CLOTHING, CLOAKS, SUITS,    **WHOLESALERS OF GENERAL MERCHANDISE**

# CATALOGUES

## How merchants ordered their stock

*This page presents a variety of japanned ware, (top) and galvanized laundry and baking pans as advertised about 1900. The japanned ware came in six different colors plus fancy gilt decorations. A set of three pieces, wholesale, was $2.00. Galvanized items came in two to six different sizes. A 10-quart dish pan, for example, (lower left corner) would wholesale for $5.30 per dozen.*

*Here is a selection of household items featured in a catalogue of 1900. Sad irons (center) were listed wholesale for $1.20 per set of three irons, one handle, and one stand.*

### CRYSTAL METAL FARM BELLS.

### STEEL ALLOY SCHOOL AND CHURCH BELLS.

### HOLLOW WARE.

Spiders and Lids.

Pots.

Ovens and Lids.

### CATALOGUES cont.

*The infinite variety offered by catalogues available to general merchants was truly amazing, and so were the prices (to later generations). A 1,600-pound school bell (above left) could be purchased for $200 wholesale!*

### LANTERNS.

 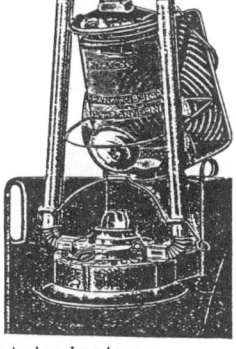

No. 0 Crank Tubular Lantern.

rass Finished, Crank Tubular Dash Lantern with Bull's Eye Globe.

lue Japanned, Crank Tubular Dash Lantern with Bull's Eye Globe.

These Lanterns are easily lighted by turning back the crank hich never becomes hot and, so does not burn the fingers.

### LAMP BURNERS.

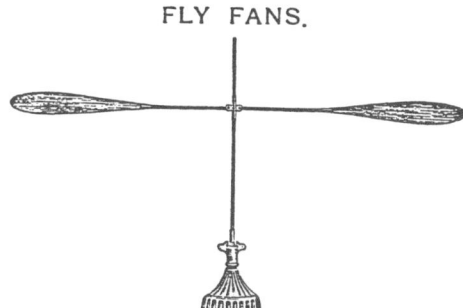

### FLY FANS.

### KITCHEN GRINDSTONES.

Style of Six to Nine Inches.

### QUEEN WALL LAMP.

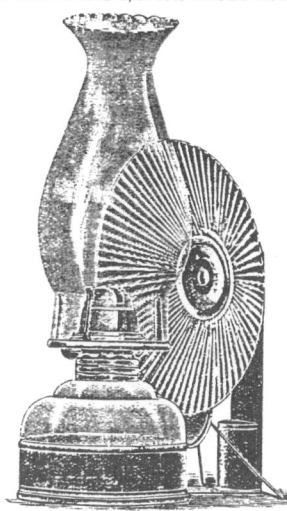

very neat and strongly made lamp, finished in brown japan.

### FLY TRAPS.

Harper.     Balloon.
Harper Fly Traps..................per dozen, $3 50
Balloon " " .............................. 3 00
One dozen in a wood box.

# HOUSEHOLD DEVICES

*Here are several "fun" items available in 1900: (1) the "only successful peach and apple parer on the market," (2) apple-only parer, (3) a "Gem" ice shaver, (4) a cherry seeder, (5) a "Gem" ice cream freezer which came in sizes from one quart to 14 quarts with wholesale prices starting at $3.25 each.*

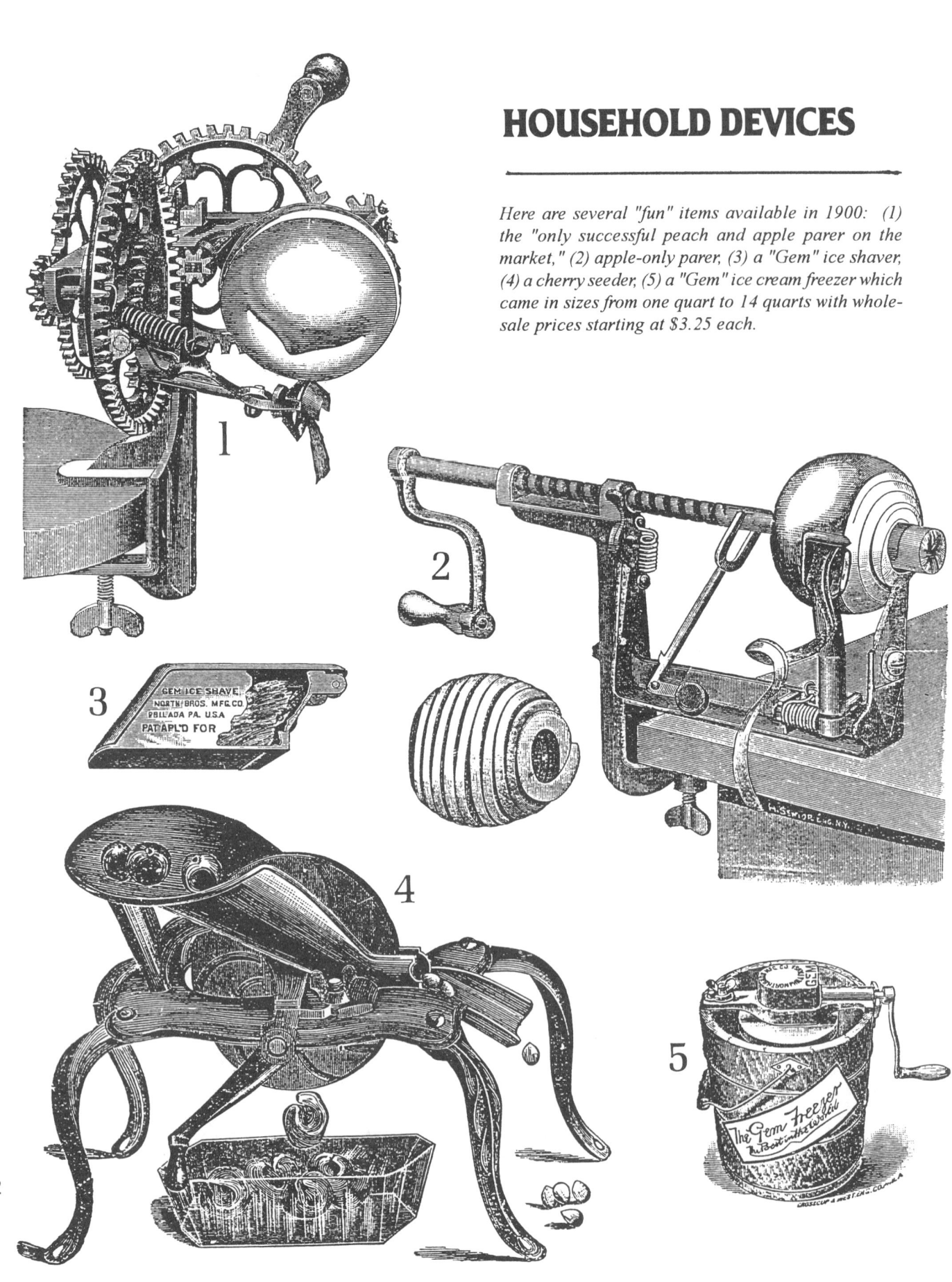

# STANDARD BRANDS OF THREAD

*The nine spools (above) represent the major producers of thread in 1891, plus a random sampling of the braids and trimmings available at the time.*

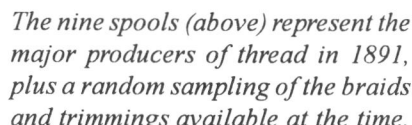

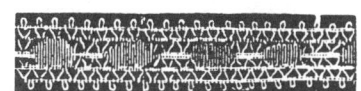

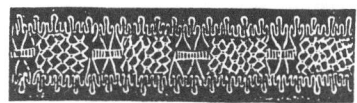

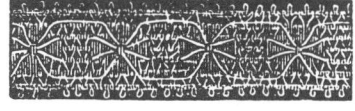

# LADIES' SKIRTS & CHILDREN'S SACQUES

# CHILDREN'S COATS & INFANTS' WEAR

# CHILDREN'S GAMES & TOYS

*A catalogue of 1891 holds a score of children's games, a selection of which is pictured below. Tiddley winks was available in three sizes, the largest at 63 cents retail. There was a popular new game available (but not shown) called "Ouija" at 96 cents retail. A special insert of wholesale prices for the merchant was missing.*

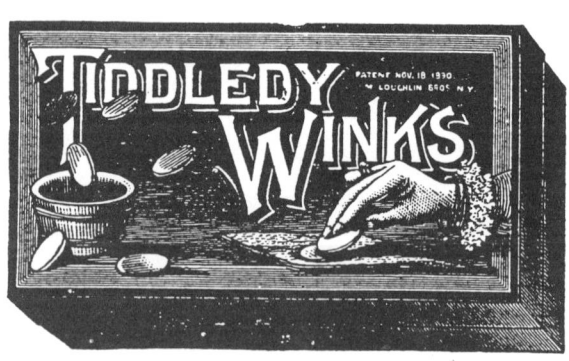
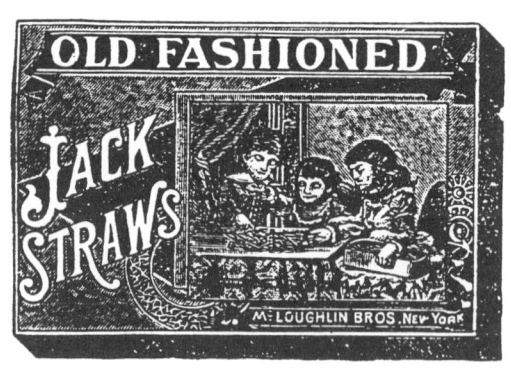
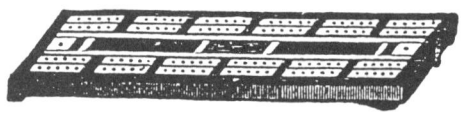

# CHILDREN'S DOLLS & BOOKS

*Below are other selections from the 1891 catalogue. There also was a "double-faced doll" with a string that, when pulled, made the doll cry. Coloring books were from 16 cents up, while story books started at 32 cents.*

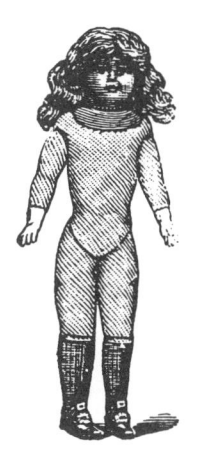

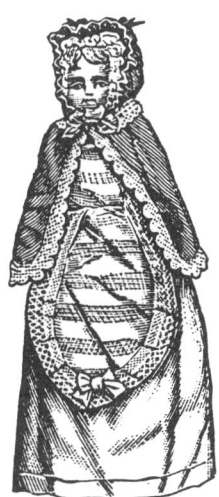

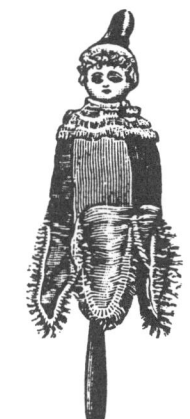

# INDEX

| | |
|---|---|
| Abingdon | 41 |
| Albemarle County | Frontispiece, 10, 30, 50, 54, 55, 57, 70, 80, 83, 90, 98 |
| Appomattox County | 52 |
| Atoka | 42 |
| Augusta County | 32, 44, 49, 56, 65, 67, 70, 93, 98 |
| Bedford County | 56 |
| Bell's Crossroads | 75 |
| Botetourt County | 41, 68, 95 |
| Bridgewater | 63 |
| Brownsburg | 39, 78 |
| Buckingham County | 48, 95 |
| Buena Vista | Contents page, 35, 68 |
| Campbell County | 45 |
| Caroline County | 95 |
| Carroll County | 91 |
| Churchville | 78 |
| Culpeper County | 51 |
| Dayton | 66 |
| Draper | 64 |
| Dunnsville | 42 |
| Essex County | 58, 60 |
| Fairy Stone Park | 89 |
| Fluvanna County | 47, 97, 99 |
| Fort Mitchell | 60 |
| Frederick County | 53, 66 |
| Goshen | 69 |
| Greene County | Cover, 45, 70, 72 |
| Grottoes | 71 |
| Halifax County | 82 |
| Hanover County | 94 |
| Highland County | 51, 57, 77, 87 |
| Isle of Wight County | 73 |
| King and Queen County | 76, 77 |
| King William County | 49, 74, 80 |
| Lahore | 35 |
| Loudoun County | 86 |
| Louisa County | 26, 51, 61, 92 |
| Luray | 37 |
| Madison County | 23, 74, 79, 86, 88, 93 |
| McDowell | 36 |
| Meadows of Dan | 46 |
| Middlebrook | 52 |
| Monterey | 69 |
| Montgomery County | 41 |
| Mount Sidney | 39 |
| Nelson County | 58, 81, 84, 87, 90, 100 |
| Nottoway County | 76 |
| Orange County | 59, 62, 81, 92, 99 |
| Port Royal | 79 |
| Prince Edward County | 38 |
| Rappahannock County | 85 |
| Roanoke County | 61 |
| Rockbridge County | 44, 47, 53, 88 |
| Rockingham County | 34, 54, 59, 91, 100 |
| Saluda | 70 |
| Scottsville | 43 |
| Shenandoah | 71 |
| Shenandoah County | 64, 65 |
| Snickersville | 40 |
| Southhampton County | 63, 92, 97, 100 |
| Staunton | 63, 67 |
| Surry | 46, 48, 82 |
| Sussex County | 33, 73, 83, 84, 89, 94 |
| Upperville | 75 |
| Washington County | 43 |
| Waterford | 40 |
| Wingina | 84 |
| Wolftown | 37 |
| Wythe County | 38 |